Praise for *Jewish Men Pray*

"Beautiful, heartfelt, uplifting … will provide inspiration and guidance to anyone seeking a more intimate relationship with the Divine. I hope this spiritually elegant book is read by people of all faiths."

—**Larry Dossey, MD**, author, *Healing Words: The Power of Prayer and the Practice of Medicine*; executive editor, *Explore: The Journal of Science and Healing*

"Offers graceful interpretations of formal prayers and creative writing of soulful 'rebbes' who transform prayer into what it is intended to be—a service of the heart."

—**Rabbi Avi Weiss**, senior rabbi, Hebrew Institute of Riverdale; author, *Spiritual Activism: A Jewish Guide to Leadership and Repairing the World*

"A rich collection…. Many men will find themselves resonating deeply with these meditations, which are certainly not for men only."

—**Harry Brod**, professor of philosophy and world religions, University of Northern Iowa; editor, *A Mensch Among Men*

"Remarkable—a book of prayers to live by and turn to in good times and in challenging times."

—**Rabbi Naomi Levy**, author, *Talking to God*; spiritual leader, Nashuva

"Heartfelt, enlightening, irresistible. Part siddur, part encyclopedia, there's something here to nourish the soul of every Jewish man. I can't put it down."

—**Jeff Levin, PhD, MPH**, university professor of epidemiology and population health, Baylor University; coeditor, *Judaism and Health: A Handbook of Practical, Professional and Scholarly Resources*

"This is not a book about how Jewish men pray; on the contrary, it is a meaningful, thoughtful, spiritually uplifting book of prayers composed by men ... for anyone and everyone who seeks to be inspired at any moment of the day."

—**Rabbi Charles Simon**, executive director,
Federation of Jewish Men's Clubs;
author, *Building a Successful Volunteer Culture:
Finding Meaning in Service in the Jewish Community*

"[A] rare book whose execution is as skillful as the need is deep. We need to learn how to pray as men and here is the guidance that will help us along this sacred path."

—**Rabbi David Wolpe**, Sinai Temple, Los Angeles, California;
author, *Why Faith Matters*

"What? Me, pray? Open this book and see if you connect. Here is help finding your voice."

—**Rabbi Joseph B. Meszler**, author, *A Man's Responsibility: A Jewish Guide
to Being a Son, a Partner in Marriage, a Father and a Community Leader*

"Beautifully done. I hope it will be used extensively by individuals and organized Jewish men's groups."

—**Doug Barden**, executive director, Men of Reform Judaism

"Gives you the most sensitive, poignant and powerful words of men at prayer. It will shatter your stereotypes and lift your soul. You'll want to bring it with you to synagogue!"

—**Rabbi Jeffrey K. Salkin**, editor,
*The Modern Men's Torah Commentary:
New Insights from Jewish Men on the 54 Weekly Torah Portions*

Jewish
Men
Pray

Other Prayer Resources from Jewish Lights

Davening: A Guide to Meaningful Jewish Prayer
by Rabbi Zalman Schachter-Shalomi with Joel Segel

*Making Prayer Real: Leading Jewish Spiritual Voices on Why Prayer
Is Difficult and What to Do about It*
by Rabbi Mike Comins

My People's Prayer Book:
Traditional Prayers, Modern Commentaries
in ten volumes
edited by Rabbi Lawrence A. Hoffman, PhD

The Art of Public Prayer, 2nd Ed.: Not For Clergy Only
by Rabbi Lawrence A. Hoffman, PhD

The Way Into Jewish Prayer
by Rabbi Lawrence A. Hoffman, PhD

Jewish Men Pray

Words of Yearning, Praise, Petition, Gratitude and Wonder from Traditional and Contemporary Sources

Edited by **Rabbi Kerry M. Olitzky**
and **Stuart M. Matlins**
Foreword by **Rabbi Bradley Shavit Artson**, DHL

For People of All Faiths, All Backgrounds
JEWISH LIGHTS Publishing
Woodstock, Vermont

Jewish Men Pray:
Words of Yearning, Praise, Petition, Gratitude and Wonder from Traditional and Contemporary Sources

2013 Hardcover, First Printing
© 2013 by Kerry M. Olitzky and Stuart M. Matlins
Foreword © 2013 by Bradley Shavit Artson

Library of Congress Cataloging-in-Publication Data
Jewish men pray : words of yearning, praise, petition, gratitiude and wonder from traditional sources / edited by Rabbi Kerry M. Olitzky and Stuart M. Matlins ; foreword by Rabbi Bradley Shavit Artson, DHL.
   pages cm
 Includes index.
 ISBN 978-1-58023-628-7
1. Prayer—Judaism. I. Olitzky, Kerry M. editor of compilation. II. Matlins, Stuart M. editor of compilation.
 BM669.J49 2013
 296.4'5—dc23

                                        2013005841

10 9 8 7 6 5 4 3 2 1

Manufactured in the United States of America
Jacket and Interior Design: Tim Holtz
Cover Photo: © Baloncici/Shutterstock

For People of All Faiths, All Backgrounds
Published by Jewish Lights Publishing
A Division of LongHill Partners, Inc.
Sunset Farm Offices, Route 4, P.O. Box 237
Woodstock, VT 05091
Tel: (802) 457-4000 Fax: (802) 457-4004
www.jewishlights.com

If to believe in God means to talk about God in the third person, then I do not believe in God. If to believe in God means to be able to talk to God, then I do believe in God.

ADAPTED FROM MARTIN BUBER (1878–1965)

To pray is to take notice of the wonder, to regain a sense of the mystery that animates all beings, the divine margin in all attainments. Prayer is our humble answer to the inconceivable surprise of living.

ABRAHAM JOSHUA HESCHEL (1907–1972)

For Miryam Tzipora Olitzky,
may all your prayers be heard on high.
KMO

For Antoinette (Rut bat Avraham v' Sarah), the
answer to my prayers.
SMM

Contents

Part II

How to Use This Book

This is not a traditional prayer book, so it is not designed to be used in place of a siddur (from the Hebrew word for "order," that is, the order of prayers), the traditional Jewish prayer book. However, it is a book of prayers, reflective of male yearning for a relationship with the Divine. Thus, it can be used in a variety of ways in traditional and nontraditional settings. If you attend synagogue regularly or infrequently, we encourage you to bring this book along with you. We also recommend that you keep it by your bedside, on the nightstand, and on your desk, wherever you might find yourself at prayer or looking for words that may express how you feel at that particular moment when you reach out to the Divine. Stick it in your briefcase or backpack. Take it with you in the car, on the train, in the subway, and on the airplane. Use it as a place to begin your meditation or to initiate your formal words of fixed prayer. There are few places where prayer—a dialogue with the Divine—is not welcome.

You can open the book and randomly choose a prayer, using the words as a way to initiate your prayer. Or you can use the table of contents and select a specific section that reflects how you feel at the moment, allowing the words to guide you. You can also browse through the book and choose a phrase or sentence that speaks to you and carry that idea with you throughout the day, allowing its sentiment to help you establish a prayerful posture for your day.

Foreword
Men at Prayer

Another book of Jewish men's prayers? What could possibly justify such redundancy? After all, the Book of Psalms is a book of Jewish men's prayers. The siddur (prayer book) is overwhelmingly a book of Jewish men's prayers. Most *piyyutim* (medieval rhymed prayers) and most liturgical poetry have constituted Jewish men's prayers. Do we really need yet another?

Let's loudly affirm the need to welcome Jewish women's voices, and joyously celebrate the growing and superb body of poetry, song, and prayers that skilled Jewish women create with such art and depth. Still, something has shifted for men in our culture. Deep tectonic changes have distanced men from their spiritual core, estranged many of us from our own deepest yearning, our own desperate hopes. In the dull cacophony of social station and the relentless grind of economic production, men have surrendered their harps, stifled their capacity to feel, forgotten to sing.

Precisely in an age in which Jewish women are finally raising their voices with renewed strength, Jewish men have accepted the muzzle and anesthetized our own sensitivity.

Resurgent Jewish women's voices deserve living respondents. Jewish men can grasp the moment to add their contributions to the living waters of Jews at prayer. The rising tide surges now, and it invites us to swim. It will not do to simply recycle the old words—as beautiful as they are—at the expense of our own outpouring. We cannot sing in someone else's voice, nor can we petition, praise, cry out, or thank with someone else's sentiment.

This lovely collection is a response to that invitation. An extraordinary gathering of men—diverse in their ages, their lives, their convictions—have convened in this collection to offer contemporary, compelling, and personal prayers. The words published here are not the recitation of established liturgies, but the direct address of today's Jewish men to *ha-Shomea Tefilla*, the Ancient One, who has always heard, and who remains eager to receive, the prayers of our hearts.

These brave Jews are bucking the tide of popular convention: they are strong, but not as Western convention portrays male strength. If warriors, then these men are warriors of mind, heart, and soul. If titans of industry, then these men are stimulating a demand for integrity, spirit, and wonder with a contemporary supply. These men are tough in courage and candor, and swift in joy, anguish, and aspiration. They are resolute in gratitude and powerful in love.

Dare we follow them into a dawning light of men who can cry and laugh, sing and dance? Of women strong and sure in their vision and their leadership? Ours is a time in which the One shines forth in new ways through people previously overlooked and marginalized. We are invited—each of us—to add our own distinctive notes to the symphony of prayer, to sing unto God a new song.

These men lead by offering their prayers, speaking for no one but themselves, yet somehow restoring to each of us our own voice. Care to join them?

Rabbi Bradley Shavit Artson, DHL
Vice President
American Jewish University

Introduction

Both editors of this book believe in prayer. Both of us have active prayer lives and advocate such a life for others. And while our personal spiritual disciplines may look different from one another to those observing us from the outside, both of these spiritual practices have the same purpose: to develop and nurture an ongoing relationship with the Divine, what religious Judaism refers to as God. Stuart's day begins in prayer-filled meditation; Kerry's day begins in a traditional synagogue *minyan*. Both are powerful and equally valid forms of Jewish spiritual expression. Both are practices that help us in our quest to lead lives imbued by holiness. And both can be enhanced by the prayers in this book.

We prepared this book to help men establish or cultivate a life of prayer, because we believe that prayer is a primary vehicle to access the Divine, to establish and maintain a relationship with that which is beyond the self, with all that is holy. And we are fearful that a life that is enriched by prayer—and the divine relationship that is presumed by it—may be slipping from the grasp of many. Prayer enhances the life of our every day. We want it to do the same for you.

Thus, this book is for those who want to start a prayer life or for those already deeply enmeshed in one. It is for the novice at prayer, as well as for the one who regularly and routinely prays according to the traditional Jewish formula of three times a day: evening, morning, and afternoon. This book is for those who pray occasionally or when spontaneously motivated to seek out a relationship with the Divine because of an event—happy or sad—in their lives or in the life of their community.

Readers may notice that this book has few explicit references to men's issues. Some might even argue that there is no need for a book of men's prayers, because the entire traditional siddur is a book of men's prayers. After all, the Rabbis who composed the traditional prayer book—and even liberal prayer books until the last quarter of the twentieth century—were almost exclusively men. And it is true that much of the material is as applicable to women as it is to men. However, the prayers in this book were intentionally composed and collected through a male lens, through the way men navigate their way in the world. Some of this navigation is explicit and easy to discern. But much of it is implicit and much more difficult to see unless you are looking for it. Thus, this is not a book of "macho" prayers. Rather, it is a book out of which men can build a relationship with the Divine.

The twentieth-century German Jewish theologian Martin Buber wrote a great deal about relationships, including the relationship between the individual and God. Buber categorized relationships as either I-It or I-Thou. The former type of relationship reflected those most of us have with inanimate objects, things that we use to enhance our personal well-being. They are things that serve us. The ideal form of the I-Thou category of relationship may best be described as covenantal, the kind that Moses enjoyed at Sinai with God. Our goal, argues Buber, is to attain the I-Thou level in all of our relationships. The "gimme" relationship that some see as their primary relationship with God will remain at its "I-It" level unless the individual strives to enter into a continuous dialogue, primarily accessed through prayer. Otherwise, people think that God is there to serve us, to provide for our needs when asked. But it is the "I-Thou" relationship that we endeavor to develop with God that should emerge as the model for the relationships we have with others, as well.

While this book is not a traditional prayer book, it can be used as a companion to any one you may find in a synagogue. It is also not a commentary on the prayer book that would serve to explain the meaning of the traditional prayers. Nor is this volume a "how-to" for traditional forms of Jewish worship. Thus, while this collection includes a brief introduction to the salient forms of prayer, its focus is on the collected prayers themselves.

You will find new prayers and old prayers in these pages. Regardless of their source or the time period in which they were written (many for this collection alone), they were written by those who are also looking to develop Buber's "I-Thou" relationship, those who affirm the importance of a prayer life for the individual.

A Prayer for Prayer

Rabbi Sheldon Zimmerman

O my God
My soul's compassion
My heart's precious friend
I turn to You.

I need to close out the noise
To rise above the noise
The noise that interrupts—
The noise that separates—
The noise that isolates.
I need to hear You again.

In the silence of my innermost being,
In the fragments of my yearned-for wholeness,
I hear whispers of Your presence—
Echoes of the past when You were with me
When I felt Your nearness
When together we walked—
When you held me close, embraced me in Your love,
laughed with me in my joy.
I yearn to hear You again.

In Your oneness, I find healing.
In the promise of Your love, I am soothed.
In Your wholeness, I too can become whole again.

Please listen to my call—
    help me to find the words
    help me find the strength within
    help me shape my mouth, my voice, my heart
so that I can direct my spirit and find You in prayer
In words only my heart can speak
In songs only my soul can sing
Lifting my eyes and heart to You.

Adonai S'fatai Tiftach—open my lips, precious God,
so that I can speak with You again.

Part I

The Purpose of Prayer in Judaism and Its Structure

Praise, Petition, and More

There are two common ways of looking at prayer, what might be described as two primary categories. The first category is called fixed prayer (*keva* in Hebrew). It is also referred to as *tefillat chovah* (obligatory or "commanded" prayers). In other words, once one enters a covenantal relationship, one takes on the requirements of the covenant, as traditional Judaism understands it. These are the prayers that make up the majority of the synagogue service, the ones you find in a traditional prayer book. It is the reason that you can go from one synagogue to another and generally find the same prayers in the same order, even if they may be interpreted somewhat differently or enhanced by different customs. The second kind of prayer is called spontaneous prayer (what is referred to as *kavanah*, or intention, but the term is also used to refer to a "sacred mantra"). This prayer category is also called *reshut* (or free prayer), those the individual may freely recite whenever motivated to do so, what is prompted by the heart. The prayers in this book generally fit this latter category of spontaneous or free prayer.

It is important to note that neither category of prayer obviates the other. They are not mutually exclusive. While fixed prayer may seem to eclipse the other in the contemporary synagogue worship service, the formal, fixed service has various places in it that are intentionally designed for spontaneous prayer. Historically, many of the prayers that are now fixed in our prayer books were the spontaneous prayers of individuals that eventually found their way into the prayer book and became fixed, because they spoke to so many people or they became the favorites of individuals compiling the prayer book.

Whether your prayers are already fixed by the Jewish tradition or they are the outpourings of the heart, a second way of grouping prayer is through its content. Thus, any prayer—whether fixed or spontaneous—might be divided into one of these three groups:

1. Petition or supplication
2. Gratitude
3. Praise

Rabbi Richard Block simply describes these groups as please, thanks, and wow. Prayer as supplication is probably the most familiar form of prayer, what people think of when they use the word "prayer." This is a fancy word for requests to God for specific things, like health, healing, or even long life. It is the kind of prayer in which the supplicant (the person offering the prayer) often attempts to make a deal with God: "If only you will do X, I promise to do Y...." In the second kind of prayers, we express our thanks for something. That's why these prayers are also called prayers of thanksgiving. They express when we are thankful for something specific: recovering from illness, surviving a car accident or a surgical operation, or the birth of a child. They can also be an expression of gratitude for something that is not tied to a particular event, such as the regular and orderly appearance of the sun, moon, and stars or even for life itself. The last kind of prayer, what is described as praise, could also be called awe. It is the experience of witnessing the amazing gifts of nature and the world around us, while acknowledging God as their source. All three of these kinds of prayer are built into the fixed prayer service, and they are reflected in spontaneous prayer, as well.

Becoming a Prayerful Person

Rabbi Lawrence A. Hoffman

We all aspire to much, and so we should. The will to become prayerful is not usually represented in the self-help books that crowd bookstore shelves. But there is very little that should rank higher in our set of expectations. We cannot hope always to avoid illness, but prayer can help us think differently about the illnesses we get. We can choose merely to hope to be good to others, or we can elect to pray about goodness and thereby become more likely to actually do the good that we intend. We can "walk sightless among miracles" of the everyday, or we can utter blessings that capture the moment and captivate the heart. We can eat our food as the animals do, or we can bracket meals with the will to do our messianic work in the window of opportunity we call our lives. We can let each day become the same as every other, or we can fill our year with the prayers evoked by the spirit of Jewish time and the consequent feel of the seasons; and thereby remain deeply human, warmly empathetic, on fire with courage, and renewed in hope. We can live in homes with nothing that is sacred, true, and noble, or we can fill our lives with prayer and blessing at every turn. We can mark time only in secular birthday parties, wishing we were not getting any older, or we can repeat at each and every occasion, "Blessed are You, Adonai our God, ruler of the universe, who has given us life, sustained us, and brought us to this season."

Becoming a prayerful person is about the choices we all make. Finding the way into Jewish prayer can be the first step on a life-changing and life-enhancing journey.

Does God Hear Prayer?

Rabbi Lawrence A. Hoffman

The traditional view of prayer is relatively straightforward. The Bible, for instance, takes it for granted that people have conversations with God the same way they do with each other. To take but one example, Moses pleads with God to pardon Israel's sins, and God duly responds, "I have pardoned, just as you say" (Numbers 14:20). Sometimes God initiates the conversation; sometimes human beings do. But either way, God appears here as an all-knowing and all-powerful being who welcomes our praise and, if we are deserving, acts positively on our requests.

By the second half of the second century BCE, the leaders whom we call the Rabbis were coming into being. So influential were they for all the rest of Jewish history that Jews today are universally rabbinic through and through.

Jewish tradition is the Hebrew scriptures that Jews call the Bible plus the voluminous writings of the Rabbis of antiquity and the subsequent equally monumental work of other Jewish leaders, also called rabbis, from the Middle Ages up to and including our own day. We customarily differentiate the Rabbis who laid the foundation for rabbinic Judaism until roughly the middle of the sixth century CE from the rabbis who are their spiritual descendants by capitalizing the first term but using lowercase for the second.

By the year 200 CE, the Rabbis had recorded their views on prayer (as on everything else) in a compendium called the Mishnah. By 400 CE, further generations of Rabbis in the Land of Israel had composed a larger work called the Palestinian Talmud. And somewhere around 550 CE, Rabbis in Babylonia (present-day Iraq) compiled a monumental work (some sixteen thousand pages in the standard English translation) called the Babylonian Talmud, or sometimes just *the* Talmud because of its size and influence. From all of these works, we see that the Rabbis viewed God more or less as had their biblical forebears. They knew that unlike the prophets, however, they themselves never heard God speak, so they concluded that actual prophecy had ceased. Apparently God didn't initiate conversations anymore.

But the Rabbis were equally certain that God still hears our prayers, and sometimes even answers them by granting the things we pray for. They were sure, in fact, that God wants us to pray—and not just as the mood strikes us, but regularly, and in community, not alone. That was an innovation beyond what biblical men and women had known. In the Bible, people pray only when they feel like it. Moses asks God to heal his sister, Miriam. Solomon requests wisdom so that he can lead his people wisely. Miriam sings God's praises to celebrate crossing the Red Sea. Hannah asks for a baby boy. But once a prayer is said, it is over and done with. No one feels the need to pray the same words twice, and the prayers don't get fixed so that other people in the same situation are obliged to copy them. The Rabbis did not question a person's right to speak directly to God with heartfelt praise, petition, and gratitude, just as biblical heroes had, but in addition, they took the next step of establishing the times and structure of a regular communal prayer cycle, the one we use to this very day. For the Rabbis, then, personal prayer was juxtaposed to communal liturgy—a far cry from biblical days, when the only public worship service had been the sacrificial cult. The God to whom the community spoke, however, was still portrayed as a personal deity who hears what people say and acts upon our words the way a powerful monarch—the Roman emperor himself, perhaps—did for powerful petitioners in court.

Most of us grew up with that kingly image of God in mind. For those of us who still believe in a God who can be pictured that way, prayer is mostly not a problem. Such a God might easily demand prayers from us, the subjects of the divine kingdom. In return, since God is all-powerful, just, and good, we might expect a positive response to our petitions, as long as we deserve it. But here is where even those who still believe in the biblical notion of a personal God run into difficulty. It is hard to prove that God really does answer our prayers, and sometimes, as when "bad things happen to good people," it is hard not to wonder why God doesn't respond the way we think a good God would.

Of late, researchers have tried to demonstrate scientifically that God hears prayer. I don't mean a simple case where a patient prays and then is healed, or even a case where friends or chaplains visit the sick and pray together with them. A positive outcome in either of these two cases may be explainable as just the impact of mind upon body: another instance where our bodily well-being is affected by our willpower, perhaps. I mean what is called prayer at a distance, whereby a random set of patients is assigned to an equally random set of worshipers, without the patients knowing that they are being prayed for. The researchers claim that the patients for whom prayers are offered have a statistically significant better chance of recovery. It follows, for these researchers, that God is indeed a personal deity who hears prayer.

That may indeed be the case, of course, but there are problems with the experiment. To begin with, it may not even be valid. It was undertaken by born-again evangelicals who were not objective observers at all, the way scientific researchers are supposed to be; they were already intent on demonstrating that a hearing God controls our destiny. In addition, however, the very concept of the experiment was flawed. How do we know, for example, that the people who were included in the group not being prayed over were not being prayed for anyway, but by someone else? Nowadays, almost everyone knows someone who believes in prayer and who is likely to offer prayer for a sick friend. The most the experiment can prove is that God hears the prayers of the designated worshipers more than those of the rest of the population—a moral dilemma for most of us, who are not ready to say that God has a penchant for the prayer of selected evangelicals but does not listen as carefully to prayers by ordinary Christians, Jews, and Muslims, for instance.

But even if the prayed-over population did get better on account of the evangelicals' prayers, it is not clear that the results would still be good news. Suppose, for instance, that without the prayers, 50 percent of the people tended to get better and 50 percent did not, but that with the prayers, 60 percent were cured while only 40 percent remained sick. What would we say to the 40 percent whom God apparently passed over? Either God would have to be somewhat whimsical, curing some but not others, or the sick people would have to conclude that they were sinners, undeserving of God's beneficence.

In other words, it may be that God really is a humanlike deity who commands that we pray, hears our prayers, and rewards the good among us. But that simple solution to the problem of prayer embroils us in theological or moral difficulties. At any rate, Jewish tradition does not demand that we believe in that sort of God. Even though the Bible and rabbinic literature regularly speak of God that way, Jewish tradition also offers us more nuanced concepts of the divine and a deeper conception of prayer that goes with them.

Tefillah / Script

Rabbi Lawrence Kushner

Prayer only sounds as if you're talking to God. In truth, prayer is reciting the words of a script evolved and evolving over the centuries that gives form to the inchoate yearnings of your innermost being. There is nothing new to say in prayer. Surely God has "heard it all before." What you need to do in order to pray is surrender your own expressions of gratitude and petition to the syntax of tradition. Only one who can allow the annulment of his or her self is capable of being transformed through the words of prayer, the lines of the script. As long as you cling to your discreet selfhood, you will be unable to transcend your self and your prayers will go "unanswered." For this reason, the key to unlocking our most important songs is the script recorded in the prayer book.

Of course, like any good actor, occasional ad libs, inflationary modifications, and even forgetting one's lines at times are part of the business. Even the sensation of impro-visation has a place, as long as you remember that your "new creation" has already been recited by the heavenly retinue since before the creation of the world. The script, in other words, is present whether or not the "play" is performed in a human prayer hall.

The Technology
of Prayer

Rabbi Stan Levy

Most of us (including me) do not believe in a (compassionate, all-knowing, all-powerful) God who intervenes in the world. So what is prayer good for? Not only do we not know the meaning of the Hebrew of our prayers, but also the English "translations" are meaningless, like "Blessed in His Name whose glorious kingdom is forever and ever." What does this mean? Then we don't know how to pray; we do not know the technology of prayer and praying. Reading, saying, or reciting prayers is not praying, just like reading a love poem is not telling someone you love to love you back. I think that I would translate each prayer with the following beginning phrase: "Oh my God ... I am so grateful to be blessed by...." "Oh my God, wow is that (this) is so awesome ... wonderful." "Oh my God ... I really need help right now ... please...."

Prayer as Art

Rabbi Ralph D. Mecklenburger

When prayer works it seems to transport me to another realm, a place where ideas and ideals come together and the world, despite its manifold problems, makes sense. I know how many wars rage around the world, but whether singing *Shalom rav al Yisrael amcha tasim l'olam* ("Grant abundant peace to Israel Your people") or reciting the Reform variation that places the onus for action on us, too ("Grant us peace, Your most precious gift, O Eternal Source of peace, and give us the will to proclaim its message to all the peoples of the earth"), I am so moved by the affirmation that the daily headlines are not the final word. Where there is God, there can be peace.

But does God truly "hear" such prayers? The personal image of God as *Shomei'a tefillah*, "Hearer of prayer," is more common but no more literal than "my Rock and my Redeemer" or "shelter us beneath the shadow of Your wings." All God-talk is metaphorical, and God is not limited or exhausted by our metaphors.

Prayer impacts us, whether or not a given worshipper believes it evokes divine response. The pious thought, the poetic language, and often the music give prayer an emotional impact. Continuing with the same example, to affirm God is to believe that there can be peace, whether God "grants" peace or *is* peace.

I call prayer "a place where ideas and ideals come together," both to echo the classic Rabbinic divine name *HaMakom*, "The Place," and to stress the interplay of ideas and emotion—for ideals are yearned-for ideas. Our spirituality, in prayer as elsewhere, is always an amalgam of the rational and emotional. In evoking emotion, touching, and activating our yearning, prayer is not theology. It is art.

The Essence
of Prayer in
Jewish Tradition

Rabbi Rifat Sonsino

In English, the verb "to pray" is a transitive verb, derived from Latin and Old French, meaning "to obtain by begging" or "to entreat." In Hebrew, the most common word for prayer is *tefillah*. It comes from the verb *lehitpallel*, a reflexive form of the root *pll*, which means "to judge." Therefore, at the very basic level, "to pray" really means "to judge oneself." When Jews engage in prayer, they look into themselves as they try to relate to the Source of all Existence: God.

Human beings have prayed since the beginning of time. They have opened their hearts to God in times of trouble as well as joy. We have records of such prayers going all the way back to the Sumerians, who inhabited the ancient

Near East as early as 4500 BCE. The Hebrew Bible contains many prayers uttered by individuals. Unlike the prayers of other religions in the ancient Near East, prayers in the Bible are directed only to God, not to other presumed intermediaries. During the First Temple period, the primary means of communal worship was a sacrifice, brought in for a variety of reasons. It is not clear whether or not prayers accompanied these offerings. Though the Bible contains a few personal prayers (e.g., Numbers 12:13; Exodus 18:10; 1 Samuel 1:11), most scholars argue that, especially during the pre-Exilic period, worship took place in silence, with priests reciting some formulas. Most of the action was on the altar. During the Second Temple period, the pattern appears to have changed. With the creation of the *maamadot* system, whereby some community representatives were present at the Temple sacrifices while the rest of the people assembled in a home to recite some prayers, formal community liturgy started to emerge. The book of Psalms, most of which comes from the post-Exilic period, contains a number of prayers stressing praise, gratitude, and petition. Our present prayer structure comes primarily from the ancient Rabbis who created many of our private and communal prayers that exist in our prayer books.

A prayer is an attempt to connect with God. It is a bridge between a person and the Divine. In the words of Rabbi Harold Kushner, a prominent author of many books on modern Jewish thought, it is "the experience of being in the presence of God." During prayer, the individual who offers up the thoughts of his or her heart is able to connect—not always, but occasionally—the inner self with the Source of all life. For, as Rabbi Burt Jacobson of Kehilla Community Synagogue in Berkeley, California, writes, "true prayer … is not just a turning inward. When we link ourselves with our own centers, with the Seed of Light within us, we simultaneously link ourselves with the One Center, the hidden Hub around which the whole universe turns."

Prayer

Rabbi Raymond A. Zwerin

Prayer. Such a simple word; such a complex concept. For many, especially for those not raised in an observant environment, prayer was baffling—thought to be the private practice of the extremely faithful or of the religious recluse—folk with whom the modern person could hardly identify. Prayer, like sex and salary, was not a subject that one spoke about in public. But the topic of late (like sex and salary) has gone mainstream. It has become the featured focus of *Newsweek* and *Time* magazine issues. Books and research papers by the dozens—no, by the hundreds—have mushroomed in bookstores and even at supermarket checkout counters. And the authors of these offerings by and large are not clerics or devotees of Eastern or Western faiths; many of these books are written by noted scientists—physicists, sociologists, researchers—who have in the main come to extol the psychological and physiological benefits of prayer.

I have been told countless times by innumerable people that they don't pray. Perfect strangers engage me in the conversation at the strangest times and under the most unusual of circumstances. It's as if I wear a sign that reads, "Talk to me about prayer." The excuses are usually interesting even reasonable. I call this the "I can't pray because ..." list.

- You know, Rabbi, I come to shul and I sit in the sanctuary, and ... nothing happens. I wish I could pray, but I can't. I don't know what I am looking for. I don't know what I should expect to happen. I don't even know if I'd recognize a prayer if it suddenly came upon me.

- I can't pray because ... I don't know that anyone or anything is listening. After the Holocaust, how can anyone believe that God really cares? I'm an agnostic, and until someone can prove that God exists, why should I pray? It's a meaningless exercise.

- I can't pray because ... the siddur is off-putting; the language is stilted; the words don't really address my day-to-day needs. I don't read Hebrew very well. I used to know it when I was studying for my Bar/Bat Mitzvah, but that was 20-30-40 years ago. I haven't read Hebrew since. I can't make heads or tails out of transliterations. I don't feel like I have a role in the service without being able to understand Hebrew. My participation feels sort of inauthentic.

- I can't pray because of the music … it's too loud / it's too traditional / it's not traditional enough / it never changes / it changes all the time / it's not modern enough / it's too folksy / it's too formal; an organ, feh / a guitar, feh / a choir, feh / what, you don't have a choir?, feh / a woman on the pulpit, feh / no women allowed on the pulpit, feh (pick any one of the above).

- I can't pray because … I have a lot of old baggage with synagogue personnel from when I was growing up. I had a miserable rabbi/cantor/principal/Hebrew teacher (pick one or more of the above) who had bad breath / wielded a large ruler / had a squeaky voice / had a big beard / wore tobacco-stained clothing / never bathed / was obsessive / threw chalk at me / didn't know how to relate / had a strange accent / didn't pay attention when I read or spoke / never understood me / was unconcerned about me as a person (pick one or more).

- I can't pray because … I am uncomfortable in the synagogue. My parents/grandparents/aunts/uncles/neighbors (pick one) were always putting down the rabbi/ the cantor/the principal/the Hebrew teacher/the dues structure. They couldn't stand the Shaprinskys—who always stuck to them like glue when they attended services. They couldn't stand the Gvertzkys—who avoided them like the plague when they saw them at services (pick one or more).

- I can't pray because … my father/mother was an atheist who disparaged prayer and called it a crock; or, they were so devout I could never match their sincerity; or, they were hypocrites who prayed only when other people were around (pick one). They kept kosher at home and ate *chazir* out / they never sent me to Jewish camp / they wouldn't let me go to Israel for junior year abroad / they wouldn't let me date Kris O'Reilly in high school / they made me go to services every week / they made me go to religious school when I really wanted to play soccer / they made me go to holiday services when they knew how much I hated crowds (pick as many of the above as fit).

- I can't pray because … I didn't have a very good religious education. In the secular world, I'm a well-trained professional. I'm a PhD in engineering / a CPA / a nuclear physicist / a renown doctor / a trial lawyer / a contractor / a computer programmer / an investment counselor / a successful business person (pick one) and I'm recognized in the secular community as an expert in my field, yet when I enter the world of Jewish spirituality I'm a klutz, a dunce, a rookie, a blithering idiot;

I feel inept, like a kindergartner—and quite frankly, it doesn't feel good.

It is the *kavanah*, the nexus, the ascendance, the reaching upward—the spiritual aspect of praying that I want to focus on: *tefillah shebalev*—that which comes not so much from the book as from the heart. Such prayer is available to everyone regardless of how much or how little one knows about the words or the techniques or the choreography of prayer. Such prayer is different from worship. Worship is what we do together as a people. Meaningful public worship depends on a community of involved worshippers. When each person in the congregation brings their personal beliefs and individual faith components to the worship experience, awesome things happen. When every person at a service readies themselves for prayer, and brings their personal expectations of what they hope to accomplish in worship into a worship service, the moment of worship can be transfixing … it can move the participants to tears.

Public worship involves a set ritual—its purpose is to unify us as a religious people. Private prayer revolves around an individual's concept of faith—its purpose is to center us as a person.

Worship is best done in the synagogue surrounded by Jews who care to be there. But there is no special place for prayer. Any place will work—a synagogue, one's home, a mountain stream, a concert hall—wherever we feel rooted and comfortable ... or, strangely enough, wherever we feel unsettled or anxious—a hospital, a classroom, a foxhole.

Now, there are things that we Jews through the ages have done to set the mood for a moment of prayer, yet no special preparation is required for the prayer moment to be authentic. These mood enhancers can include Torah study, a moment of meditation (you know, of course, that Jewish meditation techniques and practices predate every Eastern religion), certain music can set the mood, a fixed time (*keva*) can be helpful, the use of familiar Hebrew phrases or key words can serve as a mantra, a familiar prayer book, a ritual garment (*kipah, tallit, tefillin*), certain sanctuary sights (*Aron HaKodesh, Ner Tamid*, menorah), the nearness of family or friends, or just the opposite—a sense of solitude, evocative aromas, and the like. It's all of our choosing. All of it is optional. Nothing we do or have around us is mandatory when it comes to prayer. We choose what is necessary for our comfort and our stimulus.

To begin the process of praying, simply remember the words of the psalm: God is available to all who sincerely call upon God. Just start calling.

Who Can't Pray

Rabbi Raymond A. Zwerin

- Those who can't accept responsibility for their deeds—can't pray. Adam and Eve couldn't pray. "She made me eat it," he said. "The serpent beguiled me and I did eat," she said. Never once did they pray, even though while in Eden they had everything they could ever need. Therefore, in order to pray, work on accepting responsibility for your deeds and misdeeds.

- Those who will not make an effort to help themselves—can't pray. A person who expects to be cared for totally and completely can't pray. Prayer without personal effort is deemed to be evil. Prayer can never serve as a substitute for doing our own work. Nachshon first had to jump into the Red Sea ... only then did the waters part. Therefore, in order to become a pray-er, work on jumping into life with whatever energy and talent you can muster.

- A person without humility—can't pray. The prophet Micah (6:8) declares: "It hath been told thee ... what is good and what God requires of thee, to do justly, to love mercy, and to walk humbly with God." Those who always expect their way in everything can't pray. Cain slew his brother Abel because he believed his sacrifice should have been more acceptable—this is gross chutzpah, the ultimate misunderstanding of religion. Therefore, in order to pray, work on praising others before putting a shine on your own ego.

- A person who cannot trust—can't pray. Our relationship with God begins with a *b'rit*—a covenant. Covenant implies mutual regard, respect, trust that each side will fulfill its part of the bargain. Abraham, trusting God, left Ur to start a people. God, trusting the people, brought us out of Egypt. "Those who trust in Me shall not be put to shame." Trust is the precondition for prayer—just as it is for friendship and love. Therefore, at least once or twice a day, stick your cynicism in a drawer and stick your neck out on behalf of someone else.

- Persons without sensitivity, who see life and nature as if through gray glasses—can't pray. To be insensitive to the possibilities inherent in life, to be unable or unwilling to look beyond the surface of things—defeats prayer. Jacob (Genesis 28:16) has a dream.

An insensitive person would have merely seen a ladder, but Jacob realized that God was in that place. It is through our human sensitivity that we actualize God's presence—that we make God's Name manifest. Therefore, at least once a day, try to really listen to what others are saying. Take your favorite response— "Yes, but"—and put it where cigarette ashes go.

- Ungenerous people—can't pray. Selfishness is restrictive. Those who won't respond to the pain or to the needs of others—those who reach out, as it were, toward others with a limp finger—can't reach out to God either. *V'achalta, v'savata, uverachta*—when you sit at the table and eat your fill, Torah teaches, don't forget to say thank you. And don't forget those who have too little to eat, as well. Therefore, if you want prayer to come easier and more naturally, relax your death grip on your wallet and lighten up on those around you. Develop a sweeter disposition toward everyone and everything, toward life in general ... and the ability to pray will follow.

Part II

Words from the Heart

The prayers in this section represent a desire on the part of each author to connect with something greater beyond the self—what the Jewish tradition has named God. According to the Rabbis, God has many names. Each name reflects a unique way in which we can experience the Divine. Thus, there are various approaches to God in this volume of prayers. While some of the prayers refer to specific male experiences, most simply provide a male lens—through the insights of the author of the individual prayer—on the experience of the human person. Each prayer is only one side of the dialogue between what is human and what is divine.

The prayers in this section reflect an intense yearning to make a connection with the Divine. As a result of such a connection, the spiritual life of the individual can be enhanced and deepened, thereby improving one's life. A relationship with the Divine requires ongoing dialogue and what is also referred to as *kavanah*, or intention. In other words, one should try to be fully present, or as present as possible, during prayer. Try to keep at bay all of the world's noise that threatens to interfere with your prayer. Such a connection with the Divine may not come easily or the first time you make an attempt to engage the Divine through prayer. But keep at it. Such a connection has the potential to transform your life.

Yearning for God

Finding You

**Israel Abrahams, based on Solomon ibn Gabirol
(adapted from the original)**

When all within is dark,
and former friends misprise;
From them I turn to You,
and find love in Your eyes.

When all within is dark,
and I my soul despise;
From me I turn to You,
and find love in Your eyes.

When all Your face is dark,
and Your just angers rise;
From You I turn to You,
And find love in Your eyes.

Yah Ekhsof Noam Shabbat
A Shabbat Hymn

Reb Aharon of Karlin,
translated by Rabbi Zalman Schachter-Shalomi

Yah! How I long for the bliss of the Shabbat,
united in secret with Your own fervent wish.
Give way to Your own deep desire to love us.
May Sabbath in Torah be our sacred bliss.
Share Her with us who desire to please You—
Our deep thirst for union be met with delight.

Holy Presence that fills time and space!
Keep safe who keep Shabbat in their longing all week.
Like a deer that seeks water by the banks of the river,
We seek Shabbat, the secret of Your sacred Name!
Grant us all week long Her shimmering Presence,
So our hearts and our faith be pure service to You!

Warmly embrace us with Your kind compassion,
Quench quickly our thirst for Your unending Grace.
Give us the bliss drink from Eden's own river.
Your praises we sing with joy on our face.
Let Jacobs gift to us—echo all week long
Infusing our lives with a Shabbes-filled trace.

Hail Shabbat, delight of our souls and our Spirits.
Ecstasy life-throb I am awed by Your love,
Secure in Your caring there is safety and nurture—
You feed us sweet nectar from Your Source above.
As You embrace us with Mothering comfort—
In You I take refuge and pledge You my love.

A Prayer

Avrom Reyzen

Teach me, teach me how
To deal with the world, O Lord!
And how I may transform
Evil into good.
If a wild beast lurks
In our humanity,
Let me turn it toward
A mild humanity.
I've seen a trainer in
The circus tame a tiger;
Seen him de-fang a snake.
Lord, let me be wiser.
Bless me with patience, too,
And make me iron hard
That I may show [hu]mankind

Here I Am

Shye Ben-Tzur

Here I am, all yours,
Do with me as you will.
I come empty, I surrender,
My heart depends upon your grace.
Even if everything will be taken away from me,
Deep inside I will hear your voice.
From sorrow it will rouse me
And fill me with inspiration.
Here I am, all yours,
Do with me as you will.

The Innocence of My Prayers

Chaim Nachman Bialik,
translated by Rabbi Nina Beth Cardin

In the innocence of my prayers and the purity of my thoughts; in my sweet meditations and my grand sufferings, my soul sought only one thing: knowing you, just you, you, you.

Kadosh Baruch Hu

Rabbi Daniel S. Brenner

Open my lips, I whisper, closing my eyes to look for You.
But all I see is the inside of my eyelids,
screen of the 19 inch black and white television of my
    childhood,
the knob stuck on a channel that doesn't come in.

And yet, I turn to You.
Not turning really, but
I back-float and You hover above me,
I am staring out the window of the train at the seagulls
and the passing mounds of municipal waste
and You follow me like the moon.

Kadosh Baruch Hu.

That is Your name.
Not translated "holy, blessed"
but set apart, revered.

Kadosh Baruch Hu.
Set apart, revered.
It must be lonely.

Kadosh Baruch Hu,
To be alive in Your world is to be umbilical corded and
    to be belly-buttoned and to be umbilical corded again.

Kadosh Baruch Hu,
You are like a Spanish love song in which presence and
    absence
pass by one another on the sidewalk and exchange
    glances.

And speaking of music, I thank You for being just a
    song away. Birds, frogs, squirrels, bats, all creatures
    who contributed ingredients to the first human song,
    how that all happened, rhythm and melody, yeah, if
    that was what You were aiming for, wow, and even
    if it wasn't, just an unexpected byproduct, still, wow,
    wow, wow and thank you.

The things I am supposed to say to You: You gird me
    with strength, You remove slumber from my eyes,
    You support my steps, You lift me up, give me
    energy when I am weary.

What I really say before You: that there is nothing to say.

Please accept my humming and off-key melodies, my
    sighs and my silence.

And when my lips open to say:

Kadosh, Kadosh, Kadosh,

May I elevate just a little closer to Your distant and
    dreamy kingdom.

Get Me High

Rabbi Shlomo Carlebach

Lord get me high, get me high, get me high.
Lord get me high, get me higher.
Higher and higher, higher and higher …
Lord let me pray, just one prayer …
Lord let me sing just one song …
Lord let me live till the Great Morning comes.
When the whole world will sing just one song.

A Dream of Your Footprints

Avraham Chalfi, translated by Haim O. Rechnitzer

I sought You but found You not.
I sought You, enveloped in a cloud.
I filled my soul with honey from Your mouth,
I saw a dream of Your footprints in the garden.

I know that You fled far from us.
Commanded us to die perplexed.
You planted a world—our world is as a garden,
Your dream rises within it like a floral scent.

But who are You? Who? In what image are Your
    incarnations?
And what is their number in the infinite moments?
Reveal Your face to me, to the wanderer in the
    gloomiest kingdom of life.

I am Your beloved, if You are not the same as me,
and I shall not hate You, if sorrow [and weariness] are thee.
See: our daylight is impoverished sunlight.
Feel: our nights are clouds of darkness.

And empty is the space—(our window is open to see,
how empty the space is).
I sought You at night and in wind,
I sought You in heat waves
And in the dew.

Come Close
A Prayer

Rabbi Elihu Gevirtz

Ribbono shel olam,
Help me to trust You
Even when you feel so distant
Help me to know that I am on the right path
Help me to know that wherever I am, I face You
Help me to be Your servant.

Meditation Face to Face

Rabbi Elihu Gevirtz

Makom
Help me help You
Make Your presence felt in the world
Lift my face to meet Yours.
Light up Your face and shine Your light
into my heart
so that I can be Your servant.

Prayer No. 10
For Gigs

Rabbi James Stone Goodman

Master of all the worlds,
Let me be forgiving of others who irritate me—
I am sensitive, they are often not.
Or they are sensitive, when I am not.
Let me be understanding as I ask others to understand
   me.
What others think of me is none of my business.
Remind me that I am always a we,
All my teachers, inspirations, influences
stand with me at every one of my prayers and gigs.
Be easy with me, I am learning.
I am always waiting, patient in my skin.
Even if I think I know, in my bones in my blood,
I may not know.
I am waiting, longing for the water, the purest,
that issues from the rock at the edge of the world.
Out of the beauty of uncertainty, the world continues
   to exist.
And forgive me for not checking in more often.
Amen.

O Good One

Rabbi Arthur Green

O good One, whose mercies never end;
O merciful One, whose love is never simple,
We ever hope in You.

Where Shall I Find You?

Judah HaLevi

Lord, where shall I find You?
Your place is lofty and secret.
And where shall I not find You?
The whole earth is full of Your glory!
I have sought to come near You.
I have called You with all my heart;
And when I went out towards You,
I found You coming towards me.

I See You

Abraham ibn Ezra (adapted)

I see You in the starry field,
I see You in the harvest's yield,

In every breath, in every sound,
An echo of Your name is found.

The blade of grass, the simple flower,
Bear witness to Your matchless power,

In wonder-workings, or some bush aflame,
Men and women look for God and fancy You
    concealed;

But in earth's common things You stand revealed
While grass and flowers and stars spell out Your name.

Divine Expanses

Rabbi Abraham Isaac Kook, translated by Rabbi Ben Zion Bokser

Expanses divine my soul craves.
Confine me not in cages,
of substance or of spirit.
I am love-sick—
I thirst, I thirst for God, as a deer for water brooks.
Alas, who can describe my pain?
Who will be a violin to express the songs of my grief?
I am bound to the world, all creatures, all people are
    my friends,
Many parts of my soul
are intertwined with them,
But how can I share with them my light?

You!

Rabbi Levi Yitzchak of Berditchev

You!
Where I go: You!
Where I stand: You!
Just You. Again You. Always You!
You! You! You!
When it goes well with me: You!
When it goes wrong with me: You!
Just You. Again You. Always You!
You! You! You!
Heaven: You!
Earth: You!
Up: You!
Down: You!
Where I turn at every end: You!
Just You. Again You. Always You!
You! You! You!

Psalm 27

Interpreted by Rabbi Brant Rosen

You are my light my hope
why should I fear
You are my life and my strength
why do I tremble
When I contemplate surrender
to my dread
to my terror of the unknown
I hold tight to You
and Your strength gives me strength
Just one thing I ask of You
just this one thing
that I find welcome in Your home
all the days of my life
to behold Your beauty
to dwell in Your innermost place
For in You there is shelter
in times of hardship and disquiet
in Your tent there is sanctuary
from that place I will sing
a joyful song to the darkness
with openness and love
Do You hear my song
do You hear me when I cry

do not turn away
I seek You endlessly
I turn toward Your light
it seems
I've sought Your face
forever
Still in my darkest moments
this I do know
even if my father and mother abandon me
You will always be there
to gather me up
Teach me the ways of wholeness and justice
remind me that no matter how far I may stray
from this path
there is always a way to return
Even if I can't always see it
I will ever believe in Your goodness
right here
right now
in the land of the living
Hold on to Your hope
and be strong
the time of our return will soon
arrive

An Old Metaphor
"Like a moth to a flame"

Jay Michaelson

How else to express how I seem inevitably to find You:
I go on a Buddhist retreat—and find You
I dance at a gay bacchanal—and find You
In my lover's eyes, in yellow leaves,
in the most secular science—You!

So therefore I ask:
If you are going to keep drawing me close,
please,
burn me
up.

A Monist's Prayer

Rabbi Zalman Schachter-Shalomi

Y*ah*, my God where are You?
    I call You as if from afar
    and You Redeemer dwell in my heart
    so close and I know it not.
Here You are, present in my innermost
    and so too are You at the outermost edge
    both Source of mine and goal!
Where my feelings rise in me
    there are You stirring me
    nesting in the womb of my urge
Here in my eye's pupil are You
    and I yearn so much to make
    You object of my sight.

My innards would become—if only pure
    how I would scour them—
    our sanctuary in me
    sacred by Your presence
Show me how to host You,
    What a blessing!
    Your nestling in my heart

Life of my life, You are with—in me
    so how could I meet You on the outside

My song would be addressed to You
   were You beside me
   and not hidden in my voice

Zoned in the point of knowing
   You hide in unseen splendor—
   glorious as I seek Your Glory
Lingering on Your threshold
   my ego squats claiming to be
   the legal tenant of Your home.
More I cannot confuse the two
   who shimmer as one I-AMness
Never can I leave this labyrinth, my self
   by myself
Do help me sortie and free me.
   Then my prayer will be pure for You

Echo—are You the call or the answer?
   Even these words are they mine
   or Yours?
Help and tell me Love of my heart
   Are You not also
   the Love and the Heart?
Yah! God, adored One.
   I want to offer You
   a gift You will not spurn
   Your will be mine
   is it not already so?

Holy solitude, All One All-one,
    my sole One
    My soul's One my part(ner)
    My wholly—Holy Other—One
AMEN

At Dawn I Seek You

Solomon ibn Gabirol

At dawn I seek You out, my fortress and my rock,
set my prayer before You dawn and dusk.

In the presence of Your glory I stand and am afraid;
Your eye can see each thought inside my heart.

What is it that the heart and that the tongue
can do? Of what force is my spirit within?

And yet the song of man finds favor; therefore
I shall praise You while the breath of God is mine.

From Anew

Hillel Zeitlin, translated by Joel Rosenberg

Creator, great and holy, source of all who come into
the world,

You create Your world, Your child, all Your children,
once again, in every second.

Were You, for but a moment, to withdraw the love of
Your Creation,

all would turn to nothingness and void. Yet You pour
out

upon those born of You, on all Your creatures, streams
of blessing

each and every moment.

Again, the morning stars appear and sing a song of love
to You,

again, the sun goes forth in strength and sings a song of
power to You,

again, the ministering angels sing their song of holiness
to You,

again, all souls, in thirst for You, sing out their pining
song to You,

again, the grasses sing a song of yearning as they rise
before You,

again, the birds sing out a song of joy to You,

again, abandoned chicklings let out their orphan cry to
    You,

again, the trees put on their prayer shawls and lead all
    in prayer to You,

again, the fountain whispers out its prayer,

again, the poor, wrapped only in their need, pour their
    meditation out to You

their souls, their prayer, pierces the highest heavens to
    ascend to You,

again, their eyes are ever raised to You.

With but a single ray of light from You, I am
    penetrated by Your aura,

but a single word uttered by You, and I arise again to
    life,

but a single stir from Your eternal life, and I am
    saturated with the dew of youth,

for do You not create anew all that is?

Create me, then, anew, O source of life—me, Your
    child, life renewed!

Breathe into me from Your nostril's breath,

and I shall come to life anew,

the life of childhood renewed!

Psalms to You (No. 1)
Inspired by Psalm 27

Rabbi Shawn Zevit

When pressures and perspective of a cynical life
Threaten to bring me down
I ride the wave of undying faith
And its lies that finally drown
For one thing I ask, for one thing I long
To build Your house with my life
To see the beauty in every soul
And the light in every night
Hear me, Dear One, when I cry aloud
Have mercy and answer me
My heart won't rest until it shouts, "Seek My face"
And then your soul will be free
Though the world as we know it might crumble down
I know You won't forsake me
Lead me on the path of a righteous life
And I know I shall surely see that
I will long for You
Wait for You
Till eternity with You
Oh, my God.

Our Prayer

Rabbi Shlomo Carlebach

Hear our prayer, Merciful God. Let our life not be so
   empty, but let us feel that we are in
Your presence.

Why Have You Forsaken Me?

Rabbi James L. Mirel

My God, my God, why have You forsaken me?

In my time of need, I feel so alone. I want to reach out to Someone

or Something beyond myself, but at this moment, I cannot.

Help me believe in You.

I need to feel that this universe is not cold and unfeeling.

I need to sense that my pain is for some higher purpose.

Speak to me, O Hidden One.

Answer my prayers even if I speak them with skepticism.

Touch me—just a little bit—and then I will be able to overcome my doubts and embrace You in love and in hope.

Reach out to me and I will reach out to You.

When I Am Lonely

Danny Siegel

O Great and Gracious God—
when I am lonely
I imagine you to be
my favorite uncle,
lost when I was yet an infant.
Forgive me,
for I am weak.

O Great God—
when I create a sorrow
I think of you as a friend
telling tales of bears
and clever foxes,
singing stories and drying tears.
Forgive me,
I am human.

My Gracious God—
when I consider death
I call to mind a kid,
a cat, a dog, a stick,
unto the thousand eyes
of Your most certain angel—
and Your promises forever.
Love me, Lord;
I am a child.

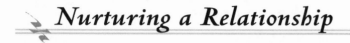

Nurturing a Relationship

"God Dwells Wherever We Let Him In" (Menachem Mendel of Kotzk)

Rabbi Adam D. Fisher

You, always available;
I, busy with distractions
try to remember You:
    the embracing wings of Your *Shechinah*
    the light of Your tallit around my shoulders
    the Heart of the universe in my heart
    Near.
Sometimes I remember
and we meet.

A Personal Prayer

Rabbi Michael Knopf

May it be Your will, Adonai my God, that I walk today
with strength and courage: to humble my pride and to
overcome my feelings of inadequacy; to find calm in
moments of rage and to summon boldness in moments
of timidity; to feel joy even in times of sadness and to
feel passionately my purpose, calling, and responsibility
in moments of excessive levity and frivolity. May I be
constantly mindful of Your presence, conscious of my
relationship with You, and empowered by Your love.
May that awareness be a wellspring from which I can
draw for the strength and courage that I need to live
better, help others, and serve You.

How Will I Convey the Great Truth?

Rabbi Abraham Isaac Kook,
translated by Yaakov David Shulman

I am thirsty! I thirst for my God like a deer alongside the streams.

Oh, who will give tongue to my hurt, who will be the harp to the songs of my moaning, who will express my bitter voice, the pain of my self-expression, broader than the broadest oceans?

I am thirsty for truth. Not to attain truth—I already ride its heavens! I am entirely immersed in the truth! Rather, my entire being is filled with anguish that comes from the painful effort to express myself. How will I convey the great truth that fills my entire heart? How will I reveal to everyone, to the worlds, to created beings, to the fullness of everything, to nations and individuals, the flashes filled with treasures of light and heat that are contained within my soul? I see them, flames rising and leaping up to the highest heavens. And how will I make others aware of it? How will I describe their power?

I am not a divine warrior, one of those mighty men who find the entirety of universes within themselves and to whom it is of no consequence whether or not anyone knows of their abundance. Their attitude is: "Those flocks of sheep that walk on two legs—what good will it do them if they know about the stature of a man, and what harm will it do them if they do not?"

But I am connected to the world and to life. People are my fellow-beings. Many parts of my soul are intertwined with them. And so how can I illuminate them with my light? Whatever I say merely covers my radiance and dims my light.

My suffering is great and my pain is great. O, my God, help me in my hurt, create means of expression for me; give me lips and speech of the lips.

Amongst the masses, I will tell my truths—Your truth, God!

Meditation before the Song of Songs

Rabbi Lawrence Kushner

So here I am, O' One I am to love with all my heart,
Waiting to be damaged by love's selflessness
or destructive through its selfishness.
Where once there was fragrance
And melody and form,
Softness and sweet,
Now only glamour remains.
Let me trust again in love's naïve ability
To restore my soul.
Let it be for me; for the one I love; for Your sake.
May the uniting of one lover with another
fashion a like union in the highest orders of Being,
Reuniting male and female dimensions
Of Your holiness.
The six days of creation
With the seventh day of Shabbat,
Sun with moon, daylight with night dark,
Insight with intuition,
Sending with receiving, having with being,
What can be told with what cannot, right with left.
Sides not only of Your holiness, but within myself.
Let me remember, One of Unity,
That all the ways of one in love

Are also the ways of Your Torah:
Affection and ecstasy,
Song and whisper,
Sharing, creating, being at once parent and child.
Surely, as it has been taught of old,
The day of the giving of the Song of Songs
Was the holiest day.
Holy One of Being, let me awaken
To the dew of my youth.
Let me be worthy to live again on the holiest day.
Let me belong to my beloved
And let my beloved belong to me.

The Whispered Prayer
Rabbi Immanuel Lubliner

No one is as remote as You, Lord our God,
yet no one is closer to us, Fatherly Ruler.

You are beyond the confines of all creation,
yet forever present in every moment.

Our deepest thought cannot grasp Your infinity
nor understand the shadow of Your glory's reflection.

But the whispered prayer,
rising from the depths of despair,
the unvoiced cry of mute needs,
the soft sigh, draining the broken heart of its sorrow,
the silent supplication of a thin, stilled voice—

All these are like great shofar blasts,
tearing the fabric of Your sphere's peace,
touching Your endlessness wherever You are.

Suddenly You, whom the utmost heavens cannot
    contain,
deign to dwell in each searching heart.

May the words of my mouth and the meditations of my
    heart
find favor in your eyes. Amen.

A Playful Psalm

Danny Maseng

Hey, you! Hey, you!
Hey, you on high—come down here you on high and I
    on low,
Down low and you are high
That's no way for you and me to be
That's no way for me to be with thee, with thou
I thought this was a two thing being one on one
Not you and me divided
My beloved is for me, you know, and I'm for you
Not me in beige and you in blue
Hey, you! What's with the distance?
What's with the attitude, your altitudiness?
Come out, come out wherever you be,
Whatever you are,
Whenever you is you was the wiz,
The one, the star!
Numero Uno, Domine Allah
You the name!
Echad, Wachad,
My Dharma essence, Brahmanescence,
Effervescence,
Rex Tremendis, holy Tatta Mamma sister spirit

Drop the veil, cause of causes
Jump the gap
Pull up a chair, a mat, a Zafu,
Make yourself at—you know,
Stay a while, what's the rush?
The similes can wait, the metaphors can pale words,
I have no words, no …
You who are beyond compare
—haven't I seen you everywhere before?
Just kidding—no, not really
Talk to me, you who never tell me anything
Let's talk … OK, I'll go, like, first
So … what's up?

A Prayer

Daniel C. Matt

May I unlearn all the familiar names that have been
   attached to You.
May I erase all the images that have been fashioned of
   You.
May I see through all the filters that have been
   imposed on You.
I yearn to discover You in all Your naked glory.
Then, overwhelmed and ravished, I will celebrate Your
   traces again and again
in all names, all forms, all being.
Blessed are You, Nameless One,
the No-thingness animating all.

On Entering the Synagogue

Rabbi Hershel Jonah Matt

1.

My God and God of my parents,
Purify my heart to worship You in honesty;
Open my lips, teach me what to say.

Let me understand where sinfully I have turned away,
    that I may now turn back to You.
Let me understand where unaware I have been blessed,
    that I may now give thanks to You.
Let me understand where I am still in need,
    that I may now ask help from You.
Hear my prayer, O God.
Send me not away empty from Your presence.

2.

Teach me, O Living God, to long for You and look for
    You
As eagerly as I crave a bit of food, a sip of water.
Teach me to know that
Without You I am hungry, thirsty, poor and all alone,
Without You life is vanity and confusion;
With You life makes sense and has a purpose,
With You I have plenty, need no more.

3.

I have entered Your house, O God,
I who am unworthy to enter.
For who may sojourn in Your tabernacle?
Who may dwell upon Your holy mountain?
He who walks before You in innocence and integrity,
He who acts with perfect righteousness,
And speaks the truth even in his heart.

How then dare I enter?

Yet You are near to all who call to You in truth,
To all whose hearts are broken and contrite.

On Creating New Blessings

Jay Michaelson

Master of the universe,
as I set my hands to compose these blessings,
I ask for Your guidance.
Grant that my motive be pure;
grant that every word I write helps me to serve You
    with love,
and helps others to serve You with love.
Stay my hand away from the temptations of the selfish
    impulse;
guard me from the urge to be dramatic, shocking, or
    reckless.
Cause my heart to incline to introspection,
where it can find You,
and remember, and write.
As Your poet said,
may the words of my mouth
and the stirrings of my heart
be acceptable to You,
my Rock and my Redeemer.

Prayer for Nature

Rabbi Nachman of Breslov

Grant me the ability to be alone;
may it be my custom to go outdoors each day
among the trees and grass—among all growing things
and there may I be alone, and enter into prayer,
to talk with the One to whom I belong.
May I express there everything in my heart,
and may all the foliage of the field—
all grasses, trees, and plants—
awake at my coming,
to send the powers of their life into the words of my
     prayer
so that my prayer and speech are made whole
through the life and spirit of all growing things,
which are made as one by their transcendent Source.
May I then pour out the words of my heart
before Your presence like water, O Lord,
and lift up my hands to You in worship,
on my behalf, and that of my children!

Unify My Desires

Jay Michaelson

Holy one:
unify my desires.
Let me look at You as I look upon a lover
and look at every lover
as I look upon You.

Psalm 11
What Shall I Bring You?

Danny Siegel

O Lord,
what shall I bring You?
What gift is there
You do not have?

Yours are chests of jewels
and endless stores of snow.
Glass and seashells
line the cases of Your palace
and the masterpieces of the world
hang all around the castle walls.

Breath and broken hearts are Yours,
and Shabbas melodies.
Help me, Lord, find gifts for You.

A caring glance, a touch, a sigh,
are these enough?
Another song, a Psalm,
do these please You?

Tell me what to bring You,
for I and all that is mine
are Yours.

Sustenance

Meditation on the *Tikkun* of Food

Rabbi Elihu Gevirtz

Holy One, Source of my breath …

I crave food, to fill my hunger.

To fill my hunger, I crave You.

Feed my body; feed my soul.

Allow me to feel awe of You that fills my heart

More than food fills my belly.

The food that sustains me comes from You

Let me eat so that my soul may serve You my holy
    Master.

For it is You that I crave.

Let me eat, conscious of You

So that I am aware that my every life comes from You

Source of my breath.

A Prayer for What I Need

Rabbi Irwin Kula

We used to pray for wine, flour, oil.
We knew the deal:
We pleased You, and asked for the things we needed.
We expected You would come through.
I still need wine, flour, and oil,
But I do not ask for them.
(The market is just down the street.)
This does not mean You are off the hook.
As I see it, the deal stands:
My coming through,
My asking for what I cannot get alone.
These are the staples:
Love, health, work, protection.
And this is what I need now: _____,
I need to have the courage to call out to You
when I am in need.
I need You to be ready to hear me.
Min ha'meitzar karati Yah, anani va'merchav Yah.
I have called You from tight places, You answered me
    with expansiveness.

LGBT

A Queer *Amidah*

Andrew Ramer

Standing before You
God of all that is
we remember
that before You created the heavens and the earth
You were One
and all was one.
Before You separated light from dark,
making day and night
You were One
and time was one.
Before You divided the waters above from the waters
    beneath,
You were One
and space was one.
And we remember
that before You created male and female in Your image
You were One
and we were one.

God of Oneness,
infinite, eternal
How queer of You to have created anything at all.
God of queerness
in whom are united all separations
we stand before You now
queer ourselves,
made of heaven and earth,
day and night,
female and male,
together
all of us
within Your awesome holy Oneness.

One person You made, God
in Your image, female and male
undivided
as male and female
are undivided in You
blended, united
You made one person only
to remind us
that all of us are one
and all of us are descendants of the same first holy
    parent.

Holy, Holy, Holy is the God of Oneness
everything that is comes forth from You.
God of our ancestors,
Abraham and Sarah,
Ruth and Naomi,
David and Jonathan,
we stand before You now and bend our knees
in awe of Your vastness.

And should we ever feel
separate
in body or soul
from You and Your embracing Oneness
we remind ourselves of the words You spoke
to one of your ancient prophets:

And let not the eunuch say, "I am a withered tree."
For the eunuchs who keep My Sabbaths,
who have chosen what I desire and hold fast to My
    covenant
I will give them, in My House and within my walls,
a monument and a name better than sons or daughters.
I will give them an everlasting name which shall not perish.

We remember and keep
Your Sabbath
we hold fast to Your covenant

we breathe into
the very first wish that You made for us

Be fruitful and multiply

And together
in our many different ways
we express our innate fruitfulness
varied as the colors of Your rainbow
refractions of one sacred light
as we join together in community
united in heartfelt prayer
in awe of Your creation
and its manifest paradoxes.

How queer of You, God
to have created anything at all.
Source of Life and Blessing,
Maker and Sustainer,
of beauty and horror
joy and blessings,
in the midst of Your world
we stand together
and call out to You
on this Shabbat
grateful
for the life that You have given us.

God of all that is
from generation to generation
we offer You our prayers.

Blessed are You
God of all that is
who queerly brought forth stars and worlds,
and placed us in the midst of them.

For You have said to us through one of Your ancient
    prophets:
My house
shall be a house of prayer
for all peoples.

And so we stand
together in this earthly house
moving into silence
awesome and holy
hoping
to find You. Amen.

Guidance for
How to Live

Guidance for Daily Living

What Do I Want?

Bachya ibn Pakuda

You know what is for my good. If I recite my wants,
it is not to remind You of them, but so that I may
better understand how great is my dependence on
You. If, then, I ask You for the things that may not be
for my well-being, it is because I am ignorant; Your
choice is better than mine and I submit myself to Your
unalterable decree and Your supreme direction.

Prayer in Time of Doubt

Rabbi Samuel Barth

Rachamana—Merciful One
I turn to seek You in moments of doubt
I yearn to find Your trace revealed in the world
I seek to find You in the Holy Place—and in the
　　outside world.
I have prayed, and studied
I have lived and loved
I have grown and built
… and I have sought for You
I have said the words
Attended the holy gatherings
Found a place among my People
Found community and friends
But I seek an answer to my question
A still small voice that my own ear can hear
A touch of the Other upon my soul
I yearn to say with truth and joy
Elohim Eli atah—O God—You are my God

Lend Us the Wit

Dr. Sheldon H. Blank

Lend us the wit, O God,
to speak the lean and simple word:
give us the strength to speak the found word,
the meant word;
grant us the humility to speak the friendly word
the answering word.

And oh, make us sensitive, God,
sensitive to the sounds of the words
which others speak—
sensitive to the sounds of their words—
and the silences between.

So Far Today

Harold Braunstein

Dear God,

So far today I've done all right. I haven't gossiped and I haven't lost my temper. I haven't been grumpy, nasty, or selfish, haven't had a sinful thought, and I'm really glad of that. But in a few minutes, God, I'm going to be getting out of bed, and from then on, I'm probably going to need a lot of help. Amen.

Lift Me Up

Rabbi Shlomo Carlebach

All Merciful, raise up the fallen tabernacle of David.
Some people need only to be shown the way. Others
need to be lifted up.

My King's Palace

Rabbi Shlomo Carlebach

Lead me back to my place, the city of holiness, the palace of my King, away from my ruins and despair. I dwelt too long in the valley of tears. Now let Your loving tenderness show me the way.

A Prayer for Direction

Rabbi Menachem Creditor

Adonai, please teach me how I can heal both myself and those around me.

Help me choose the path that I am to walk, and guide my footsteps so I will not stray.

Show me where I am needed, for that is where I want to be. Though I sometimes may desire to take the easiest route, help me to understand that boulders in the path can be part of my growth.

Though I may make mistakes, help me to accept criticism and correction, and turn me from temptation lest I stray from a holy path.

Give me strength, Adonai. Help me rediscover my health, happiness, and life. Protect me, Sustain me, and Help me feel both satisfied and full of healing power.

Everyday Miracles

Rabbi Abraham Joshua Heschel

I did not ask for success;
I asked for wonder and You gave it to me.

Based on Moses Maimonides's Prayer for Physicians

Rabbi Jeffrey Goldwasser

Almighty God, You created all reality with words, and You have endowed Your creations with the wisdom to express their deepest thoughts and the stirrings of their hearts with words. You have blessed humanity with language, which contains within it the secrets of creation and which allows us to understand Your presence in all that we experience and all that we do. As You endowed Bezalel with a divine spirit of skill, ability, and knowledge to create designs for the Tabernacle in the wilderness, may You give me a portion of Your creative spirit.

On this day, allow me to express myself with wisdom and modesty to bring beauty into the world and to reveal Your truth through words and design. Guard me against using words that bring harm, that spread gossip or slander. Grant me the judgment not to use language, which is Your creation, as a weapon of falsehood. In all that I do, allow Your aspects of beauty and truth to flourish.

Preserve the strength of my body and of my spirit to do Your will in peace. Imbue my soul with gentleness and calmness when others judge me. May even this be of help to me, for others know many things of which I am ignorant, but let not the arrogance of others give me pain.

Let me be contented in everything except in my growth to understand, live, and express Your will. Never allow the thought to arise in me that I have attained sufficient skill, but give me the strength, time, and energy always to extend my ability. For art is great, but the mind of a human being is ever expanding.

Almighty God! Support me so that my work will be of benefit to humanity, for without Your help not even the least thing will succeed.

Your Guiding Power

Rabbi Sidney Greenberg

Lord, Your word brings on the evening twilight;
The heavens proclaim Your glory

And we, Your creatures on earth,
Behold in wonder Your endless miracles.

Help us to recognize Your guiding power
In distant galaxies and in our own souls.

Teach us Your law of righteousness and love
So that Your spirit may govern our lives.

Father of peace, bless our worship;
May our meditations find favor in Your sight.

May our gratitude for Your wonders
Lead us, in love, to Your service.

So that, like the changing seasons, the days, the nights,
Our lives, too, will proclaim Your glory.

Yearnings

Rabbi Jules Harlow

So much this past year has threatened
To break my spirit. Help me, O Eternal,
For I have been very low.
I stand here, weary,
Empty and dry.
In thirst and hunger I stand,
Seeking comfort, even joy.
Transform my sorrow, Eternal;
Help me to renew my faith, my hope,
As I raise my soul toward You....
Open Your lips within us, Eternal One,
That we may speak Your praise.

Inspired by Psalm 8:6

Rabbi Hayim Herring

The Psalmist sang that
we are a little lower than the angels,
and higher than the beasts.
But we know that we have the capacity
to be lower than the animals
and higher than the angels.
Help me, God, remember that every thought, every
   word, and every action
is a decision,
to enhance or diminish the animal or the angel.

Open Up Our Eyes

Cantor Jeffrey Klepper

Open up our eyes, teach us how to live
Fill our hearts with joy and all the love You have to
   give.
Gather us in peace as You lead us to Your name
And we will know that You are one.

Holy One ... My Heart Is Heavy

Rabbi James L. Mirel

Holy One ... my heart is heavy.
My daily existence has become a source
    of deep sadness and disappointment.
Give me the strength to face conflict
    with dignity and forthrightness.
Let me speak openly, but with compassion.
Give me the patience to hear the opinion of others
    without being defensive or overly sensitive.
Help me discover the true nature of this conflict
    and then act in an appropriate manner.
Help me distinguish between matters of principle
    and matters of power.
Let me be understanding of others' shortcomings—
    and of my own.
If, after making the best effort I can, I am not
    succeeding, help me remove myself
    from a situation without bitterness or anger.
Help me refrain from pettiness or recrimination.
Help me remember that I am created in Your image.

A Prayer

Rabbi Nachman of Breslov

My God,
I work and I strive,
never knowing
if I will succeed.
You and only You
can give hope to my dreams.
With Your help
I am spared
wasted efforts.
With Your blessing,
all the hardship I endure
can bear fruit.
You and only You
are the key to success
in all that I do.

Ana B'Koach

Translated by Rabbi Zalman Schachter-Shalomi

Source of Mercy,
With loving strength
Untie our tangles.
Your chanting folk
Raise high, make pure
Accept our song.
Like Your own eye,
Lord, keep us safe
Who seek union with You!
Cleanse and bless us
Infuse us ever
With loving care.
Gracious source
Of holy power!
Do guide Your folk.
Sublime and holy One,
Do turn to us
Of holy chant.
Receive our prayer
Do hear our cry
Who secrets knows.
Through time and space
Your glory shines,
Majestic One.

God Consciousness

Rabbi Elie Kaplan Spitz

Ribbono shel ha'olam, Master of the universe,
In talking to You, God, I am without words because
   ultimately God's knowledge is not my knowledge—
   and yet,
You have placed within me the seed of Your
   consciousness.
May I use Your presence to serve the world that You
   created. May my heart be open and compassionate.

May I be your servant. Amen.

Mindfully Alive
Ten Short Prayers

Rabbi Elie Kaplan Spitz

Ribbono shel ha'olam—Master of the revealed and the
hidden,

May I delight in the unfolding kaleidoscope of Your
creation.

May I use all my senses to breathe in, feel, and taste,
the glory of One.

Grace me with the patience and imagination to see in
a leaf's veins my own pulsating hand and Yours, too.

May I connect with each piece of Your creation as
family.

May I value those that I love for their precious mystery.

May I respect the differences apparent in others and
embrace our commonality.

May I honor those yet unknown as potential friends.

May I listen with greater humility, empathy, and
wisdom, hearing your voice expressed in the speech
and unspoken words of others.

May my mind undermine false beliefs so as to see the
world more clearly, honestly, and lovingly.

And may You guide me to craft understanding as a
sturdy staff for the journey ahead,

Walking with You and exuding compassion as Your
hands, eyes, ears, heart, and pockets.

Before and After I Pray

That We May Pray Well

Rabbi Elimelech of Lizhensk,
translated by Rabbi Zalman Schachter-Shalomi

Yah, our God,
You are our parents, God,
You are open to hear our pleading prayer
with compassion.
You give a caring ear
to what Your people Israel is crying for.
This is our prayer to You,
please grant it.

Open our hearts,
focus our thoughts,
help that our prayers
may flow freely from our lips
and incline Your ear to hear
how we, Your servants,
are seeking Your favor,
crying in a pleading voice
and with a shattered spirit.

You, kind compassionate One,
God of infinite mercy!
Please forgive us, pardon us,
and atone for us
and for Your entire people,
the house of Israel,
so that whatever we have failed
to do right
or what we have done wrong
or when we acted in ways
that are wicked
and rebelled against You
be forgiven, pardoned, and atoned
for us and for Your entire people,
the house of Israel,

How well You know,
and it is apparent to You
that it was not with malice or willfulness
that we transgressed what You teach us,
what You command us
in Your Torah and commandments.

In our bellies
there burns a fire without ceasing,
a *yetzer hara*, the drive of selfishness
which draws us

to the vices of this world
and its follies.
The *yetzer* confuses our awareness,
even when we stand before You
seeking to pray and plead for our lives.
The *yetzer*'s incitement
constantly confuses our thoughts
with all sorts of thoughts and schemes.
We cannot resist it;
for our awareness is uncertain
our mind unsteady
the troubles and preoccupations
of making a living
under times of oppression
bear down heavily on us.

Therefore, You,
who are compassionate and kind,
fulfill for us what You promised
to Moses, Your faithful servant,
when You said,
"I will favor whomever I will favor
and I will be compassionate
on whomever I will be compassionate."
And this You had our sages tell us.
This applies even to those

who are not worthy
for this is Your way;
to be kind both to those who are bad
and those who are good.

It must be obvious to You
how we are troubled
how hard our life is
and what we must bear—
it is so difficult for us
to come near to You
and to serve You well,
to have our feelings be sincerely
in harmony with Your will.
Dear Father in heaven!
What pain we feel in our souls!
Please arouse Your mercy and kindness
freely and abundantly
and banish, erase
our attraction to evil.
Let not our evil *yetzer*
be active in our innards.
Let him not seduce us
let him not deflect us from serving You.

May no evil schemes arise in our heart
when we are asleep or awake

especially at that time
when we stand in prayer before You
and at times
when we study Your holy Torah
at times when we are busy
fulfilling Your commandments.
Then let our thoughts be pure and clear,
our own awareness steady and strong,
sincere and heartful
as You would have us be.

Awaken in our hearts
and in the hearts of all of Israel,
Your people
the aim to unify You
in all truth, in all love
so to serve
as to be pleasing to You.

Fasten such steadfast faith in You
to be deeply anchored in our hearts
not to vacillate from it.

Remove from us all the barriers
that separate us from You,
our Father in heaven.
Save us from stumbling on our path,
Keep us from going astray.

Don't forsake us,
don't abandon us,
keep us from being disgraced
before You.
Be present to us
in the words of our prayer
and in the work of our hands
as they serve You
and the thoughts of our hearts
as we think of You.

Please, our Father in heaven
in Your abundant kindness
Grant us the boon
that our thoughts
and words and actions,
all our motives and our feelings
those we are aware of
and those we are not aware of
those that are manifest
and those that are hidden
with all of them together
be unified in sincerity and truth
without any self-deception.

Purify our hearts,
sanctify us,
sprinkle us with cleansing water
to purify us,
wash us clean
with Your kindness and love.
Plant Your steadfast love,
and Your awe in our hearts
at all times
and in all places
as we go about our lives
when we lie down and get up;
that there always be Your Holy Spirit
ardently active in our innards
that we may rely on You always,
on Your greatness,
Your love and Your awe.
May we be securely anchored
in Your Written and Oral Torah
in the part of the Torah
that is open to all
and the part of Torah that is hidden.
In doing the *mitzvot*
may we unify Your awesome name.

Protect us from hypocrisy,
from pride, anger, and vindictiveness
from depression, from tale bearing
and other vices.
Protect us from everything
that might damage
the holiness and purity
of our service to You, whom we love.

Pour out the Holy Spirit over us
that we stay close to You,
that our longing for You
grow and increase.
Raise us up from rung to rung
that we might come close to the rung of
our holy forebears
Abraham, Isaac, and Jacob
may their merit protect us.
In this way,
You will always receive our prayer;
You will always answer us
when we pray for anyone
be it a single person
or the whole people Israel.
May You take joy in us.
May Your glory be reflected in us.

May our prayers bear fruit
and be fulfilled, above and below.
Do not attend to our flaws,
especially the sins of our youth,
as King David peace be upon him said,
"My youthful sins in my rebellions
do not keep in Your memory."

Please, turn our sins
and rebellions into merit
that there flow to us
from the realm of repentance
the challenging call
to return to You wholeheartedly
and to repair all that we have damaged
of Your pure and holy names.

Rescue us from envy.
Let not jealousy
of any person arise in our hearts
and let not others be vindictive to us,
on the contrary,
place into our hearts
appreciation for the goodness
of our fellow beings
let us not seek to find fault with them.
May we speak to each person

with civility and gentleness.
Let not hatred arise from one to another.
Strengthen us
that we might love You more
for You know well how our intention is
that it all should bring You
pleasure and joy,
for this is the roots of our intention
despite the fact
that we don't have a strong enough mind
to keep the aim
of the *kavanah* of our heart
focused on You.
Enlighten us so that we might learn
to fully know Your good purpose.
This is what we plead to
You, all merciful God.
Please accept our prayer
in compassion and goodwill.
Amen, let this be so willed by You.

Following the *Amidah*

Mar the son of Rabina

My God, keep my tongue from evil and my lips from speaking guile. May my soul be silent to those who curse me, and may my soul be as the dust to all. Open my heart in Your law, and may my soul pursue Your commandments, and deliver me from evil, from the evil impulse and from all evils that threaten to come upon the world. As for all that design evil against me, speedily annul their counsel and frustrate their designs! May the words of my mouth and the meditation of my heart be acceptable before You, O God, my Rock and my Redeemer!

Psalm of Dust

Danny Maseng

Guard my tongue from evil
And my roar from dimming even slightly;
Guard my lips from speaking falsehoods
Even though the truth is what can really maim;
And to those who curse me—may my soul be silent
And my heart roar beneath the surface of my burning
   eyes;
And my soul shall be as dust, as earth
For, before and under everyone;
For a blessing,
For the benefit of strangers everywhere,
Especially the ones I'll never get to know;
May my soul be fertile ground
Compassionate, passionate ash of lion
Turned to mead,
A shadow of myself, a trace of silt and honey;
Open up my heart and guard my gates
My eyes, my comings and my goings
Once the gates are opened can the lion be contained?
Chase me with your teaching
Pursue me till my breath falls heavy unto you,
Draw me near, subdue me with that thing you say is
   love

I have nothing but your word for it,
I have nothing but these ramblings that I utter
May they be of use to someone;
May the meditations of my breaking heart be
    acceptable before you
My hidden rock
My luminous,
Unyielding
One

I yield

Cleanse Me

Rabbi Hershel Jonah Matt

O cleanse me from all self-righteousness and conceit.
Teach me how in humility to speak to You,
And how to listen.

Before I Pray

Louis Newman

> Creator of life and goodness and truth, today and every
>   day grant me—
> the courage to speak honestly and the humility to ask
>   for help when I need it.
> "It has been told you what is good and what the Lord
>   requires of you—only to act justly, to love mercy
>   and to walk humbly with your God."
> May I never give in to temptation or waiver in my
>   commitment to
>   soul-reckoning.
> "Who will ascend the mountain of the Lord and who
>   will stand in God's holy place?
> The one who has clean hands and a pure heart, who
>   has not sworn deceitfully and has not dedicated
>   one's soul to vain things"
> —and may I know the serenity that comes with purity
>   of heart and integrity in all that I do.
> "Light shines for the righteous and joy for the upright
>   of heart."

Before the *Amidah*

Rabbi Neil Sandler

I need some help here, God. I need some help with sincerely and mindfully opening my mouth as I turn to You. Help me.

Following the *Amidah* in *Siddur Nusach Sfarad*

Translated by Rabbi Neil A. Tow

May it be Your will, Adonai my God, God of my ancestors, that the *kinah* [jealousy/anger] of others not impact me and that my jealousy/anger not impact others. And may I not become angry today and not anger You. Save me from the *yetzer hara* [evil inclination] and place submissiveness and humility in my heart. Our Sovereign and God, make Your name One in Your world, build Your city, make foundations for Your house, complete Your sanctuary, bring in the exiles, free Your flock and give joy to Your people.

Getting Started

Help Me to Start
Based on Psalm 116:25

Rabbi Shlomo Carlebach

I beseech You Lord, help me to start anew. I beseech You Lord, let me succeed to try again if I fail.

Help Me to Become

Rabbi James L. Mirel

Blessed are You, Eternal One our God, Holy Presence in the Universe, You are the force of all Creation that makes possible the transformation of life, my life, from mundane to holy. Help me to become all that I have been created to become.

Prayer for the New Year

Rabbi Dov Peretz Elkins

I pray that the new year will bring our people one step closer to the ideal of a nation of students and a people of prophets. That Jewish learning will be the daily practice of every Jew young and old; that books be more treasured than clothes, ethical maxims better known than bank balances, and moral laws more significant than market rules.

That learning how to live becomes as important as learning how to earn a living. That we have as many Hebrew scholars as we do Hebrew physicians and dentists. That we spend as much time reading as eating.

I pray that God heal the deep rift in the heart of the world that divides north from south, east from west; that persons who are white, black, yellow, Jew, Christian, Buddhist, or Muslim see in each other only the spark of God and the soul of humankind.

I pray that prejudice and discrimination be considered as sinful as murder, as odious as shaming God; that denying someone an education, a job, or a home be a custom expunged from the American heritage.

I pray that the basis for human love will change from the color or one's skin to the size of one's heart.

Now Is the Time for Turning

Rabbi Jack Riemer

Now is the time for turning.

The leaves are beginning to turn from green to red and orange.

The birds are beginning to turn and are heading once more toward the south.

The animals are beginning to turn to storing their food for the winter.

For leaves, birds, and animals turning comes instinctively.

But for us, turning does not come so easily.

It takes an act of will for us to make a turn.

It means breaking with old habits.

It means admitting that we have been wrong; and this is never easy.

It means losing face; it means starting all over again; and this is always painful.

It means saying: I am sorry.

It means recognizing that we have the ability to change.

These things are terribly hard to do.

But unless we turn, we will be trapped forever in yesterday's ways.

Lord, help us to turn—from callousness to sensitivity,
    from hostility to love,
    from pettiness to purpose,
    from envy to contentment,
    from carelessness to discipline,
    from fear to faith.
Turn us around, O Lord, and bring us back toward You.
Revive our lives, as at the beginning.
And turn us toward each other, Lord,
    for in isolation there is no life.

A Prayer

Rabbi Shneur Zalman of Liadi

Dear God—You commanded us that we should "know today, and put it back into our hearts, that You are God—in Heaven above and Earth below—there is nothing else," and I'm asking You to help me, to keep my mind really clear, that I might see Your workings in the universe, to feel that You are the life that is invigorating me in this very moment.

The Sun and the Rain

Danny Siegel

As the sun in its rising (Your divine creation)
gives us hope—give us hope.
As the rain in due season (Your handiwork)
gives us sustenance—sustain us, O God.
Give us confidence and faith
as Noah when he saw the rainbow
You set in the heavens, touching the earth
after the storm.
As, in Your wisdom, You have given us the rose,
the iris, blossom of cherry trees and plum—
give us beauty in our lives.
And as the sun in its setting (by Your word)
give us peace of mind and healing.
Set us free from pain and doubt.
As the waves rise and fall—set in motion by Your will—
restore our strength to share Your vision.
As of old, renew our hearts so we may serve You
as You would wish.

Give Me a Quiet Heart

Rabbi Rick Sherwin
Based on a prayer by Rabbi Chaim Stern

Give me a quiet heart, and help me to hear the thin voice of silence within me. It calls me to reflect the Divine Image in which I am created. It teaches me to do my work faithfully, even when no one's eye is upon me, so that I may come to the end of each day feeling that I used its gifts wisely and faced its trials bravely. It counsels me to judge others less harshly and to love them more freely. It persuades me to see the divinity in everyone I meet and to see that same divinity within me.

Psalms to You (No. 2)
Inspired by Psalm 22

Rabbi Shawn Zevit

I cry by day, but You don't answer
Numbed at night, I hear no laughter
My God why have You left me?
Oh, my soul is poured out like water
My heart's like wax, it's melting over
My God why have You left me?

Others have been here—I know they have trusted
Others have hung in and not been disappointed
Others cried out and found a way through the forest
But what of me? My God!

Don't be so far when trouble's so near
Why does it hurt so, why do You disappear?
My God why have You left me?

You claimed my heart since its very first breath
You've been my God, and will be 'til my death
In the silence, I listen for Your help
Save me now from a hardened heart

Why have You left me? Why have You gone so far?
Shut Your ears to my anguished roar
My God why have You left me?

Let the ends of the universe turn around
Open Your souls and soak in the sound

It's a greater love than you have ever found
God has acted,
look out now,
God in action
My God!

For the Community

Here I Am: *Hineni*

Rabbi James Stone Goodman

Here I am
planted in front of You and in front of my fellow
    conspirators in prayer, to pray for myself and on
    behalf of my community,

Some of the people here I know—
I love them.

Some of the people here I don't know—
I love them too.

Remind me to empty myself
of all that separates me from You
and from everything I love the most—
I am a vessel, an instrument of your will.
Play me like a harp a flute an oud.

Help me to empty myself—
to be a vessel, an instrument.

Help me to empty myself of that combative Detroit
    "get out of my face" or I'll wipe the floor with you

attitude [substitute here your own obstacles and
when you do, take a moment to name them:
what is it that separates you from God
and all you love the most?].

As for me,
let me love as purely and as wholly as
I want to and as I know I can.

May our prayers
our actions
our lives
be rescued from the externals.

Let all our prayers rise
uninterrupted like doves
straight to heaven,
let us be guided to
the sacred heart of the world,

Let us never lose our yearning for
peace, depth, and beauty,
let us honor our fathers and mothers,
our grandfathers and grandmothers
all our holy ancestors
who rest at the foot of the
Throne of Glory,

With our prayers
our actions
our songs
today and all days,

Let us remember that nothing
nothing in God's creation is ever lost,

And everything
every single thing
is going to be
all right.

Bless us,
O God
The One God
The unclaimed God,
Bless us.

Amen.

A Prayer for All Occasions

Translated by Rabbi Zalman Schachter-Shalomi

Our God, our parents' God
You hear the prayers
of our pleading
of all of us who turn to You.
May it please You
to hear also my own prayer.
I approach You and plead with You
Knowing well
that I come without merit and worth
and without worthwhile deeds
I am embarrassed to raise my face to You
To pray for myself and for other people—
yet, it is Your boundless
compassion and kindness
that encourages me to trust
that You will not scorn me
but that You will support me
and come to my aid.

May my poor song
be pleasing to You
in hearing our prayers with compassion.
I come with a sore heart
to plead with You

Please, in Your great compassion
take pity on the remnant
of Your people Israel
help us all and extricate us
from our confinements
save us from our oppression
help us to leave poverty and humiliation behind
and keep us from a scarcity mentality
help us from all kinds of ruinous happenings
erupting upon the world.

Those who are healthy among us
Your people Israel
guard them that no illness befall them,
no suffering enter them, *chalilah*!

Those, among Your people
the house of Israel who are ill
hasten and send them a complete recovery.

Release all hostages to freedom
and save our people the house of Israel
from all pain and damage, assaults and accidents.
Compassionate One save us from such.
Childless couples,
bless them with vigorous children,
proper, good, and kosher offspring,

that are well thought of by You
and all the children of Your people,
may their parents
their fathers and their mothers
merit to raise them
to study Torah and to serve You, God
so that they might walk in a straight path
and be attuned to awe of You.
Let no childhood disease take hold of them.
May they be protected
from demonic influences
and from ill winds in the world,
from plagues and accidents,
so that they might be healthy and wholesome
involved in serving You
and studying Torah all their lives.

Those mothers to be
who are carrying new life
make them carry to term
in peace and without pain.
When the time for their birthing comes
protect them from all hurt and damage
help them through labor with ease
and without any complications.

Above all, may Your great mercy protect
the exiled people Israel,
and the remnant of Your holy Torah.
May all who oppress them
become aware of Your retribution
and not shed innocent blood.

And those of Your people Israel
who have gone astray—
may they find ways to approach You again.
Receive them in complete *t'shuvah*.
Your right hand of grace
is stretched forth
to welcome those who repent.
Send us Your life and Your truth,
to guide us to live up to Your intention
in great compassion
help us to come home
and redeem us with a lasting redemption.
Amen *selah*!

Prayer for Our Nation

Rabbi Daniel G. Zemel

Dear God,

We love our nation deeply—from sea to shining sea.

We are inspired by the beauty that You have bestowed upon this land from the rocky soil of New England to the Pacific beaches of California, from the snow-covered peaks of Alaska to the deserts of the Southwest. May we as a people learn to preserve the glory of this earth.

We are likewise inspired by another beauty—from the lady who lifts the flame above New York Harbor to the memorials at Valley Forge, Lexington, and Concord— from the artistic wonders of the National Gallery to the public museums and libraries that fill our cities and towns. May we as a people preserve these treasures and keep them open and accessible so that all may learn and grow from their riches.

On this Holy Day we thank You for those men and women, soldiers, sailors, and marines on ships and bases far from home who stand at risk in order to watch and guard over our liberties and our lives. They too are a national treasure, and we ask for Your vigilance and blessing upon them.

May we as a nation be guided by Your wisdom to rediscover and renew the sacred flame of our American heritage, which so many have given their lives to safeguard.

In these days of economic struggle—we thank You for the bounty You have bestowed upon so many, and we ask that You guide with strength those with plenty—to offer not only a generous charitable offering but also a real hand up to those with the least.

In this season we invoke the words of Your prophet Malachi, who besought You in prayer as One who could turn hearts. Let the wounds of separation and division be healed by turning all of our hearts to listen to the truth—no matter the source, allowing us to find a higher truth that includes us all.

May we learn to honor our diversity and differences as a people, even as we deeply recognize our common humanity.

Bless those men and women who lead our nation, and endow them with courage, compassion, and wisdom.

May our leaders then inspire us all to work to create a new spirit of caring, honesty, and plain good character.

May we as a nation rededicate ourselves to truly living as one nation, under God, indivisible, with liberty and justice for all—just like they teach it in the civics books.

On this Yom Kippur—our holiest day as Americans and as Jews, we humbly ask these blessings of You, our Creator.

A Man's Role

May God Protect You
For My Son, a Marine Infantryman

Rabbi Mordecai Finley

May God protect you, guard you, and keep you from
any harm. If you should find yourself in danger's path,
may God bring you back whole of mind and body to all
those who love you. May the honor and courage within
you guide you as you serve your God, your people, and
your nation.

Children

Rabbi Nachman of Breslov

Loving God,
what is more precious
than our children?
Is there any treasure that can be
more beloved,
more pure
than those cherished souls
we have brought into the world?
Help me guide them well,
dear God,
and help them accept my guidance.
Help them lead their lives
with faith,
wisdom
and truth.

A Father's Prayer

Rabbi Jesse Olitzky

Avinu shebashamayim, our Father in heaven, give me the wisdom, insight, courage, and strength to be a father. You have blessed me with a child, one of Your divine creations, made in Your divine image. You have blessed me with fatherhood; now show me how. You who have provided for me my whole life, You who continues to provide for all my needs, give me the strength to provide for my daughter, strength when I am weary from sleepless nights of teething, sleepless nights of slumber parties, sleepless nights of staying out past curfew. Bless me with the wisdom to discern between tears of joy and tears of sorrow, the ability to heal a sore throat and a broken heart, the humor to make my daughter laugh with me and at me, the self-discipline to discipline her even when it eats me up inside. Lord who walks with me, allow me to walk in Your ways, so that she may walk in Your ways, to live a life full of the ethics and values that I want her to hold dear, to discern between right and wrong so that I can teach her the difference. Just as I hope and pray that You will bless her and protect her, permit me to bless and protect her. Most of all, my Strength, when I am not there, provide my child with the strength to protect herself, and protect others as well. Permit her to recognize the divine spark within her so that she may cling to You.

A Prayer for Parenting

Rabbi Simkha Y. Weintraub

Parent of All:

You have blessed us with children,
  with the *b'rit*/covenant of parenthood,
  with deep reservoirs of love, concern, responsibility,
    and guidance.

Thank You, Close One,
  for the astounding privilege of parenting;
  for discovering capacities we had not known in
    ourselves;
  for the blessings of health, safety, discovery, joy,
  and love for, and from, our children and all children;
  for opening our minds with curiosity,
    our hearts with compassion,
      our communities with care.

Help us to emulate the care of your *Shekhinah*:
  To listen well and to respond sensitively;
  To be open and flexible, or clear and unyielding, as
    necessary;
  To maintain boundaries and yet to extend ourselves
    in some new ways;
  To know when to speak and when to be silent;
  To speak truth and match our deeds to our words;
  To rely on profound beliefs and hard-earned
    knowledge,
      but also to be able to take risks if required;
    To have faith in ourselves and in our world
      so that we can do what is needed;

To maintain hope and vision when the challenges
    before us are so hard.

When we are wracked by worry,
    Help us reach for calm and equilibrium.
When we find ourselves confused and lost,
    Open for us Your Torah and the Torah of loving
        parents' lived experience.
When disappointment, frustration, or rage mount
    within us,
    Enable us to keep perspective, consider different options,
        and channel the energy toward relationship and
        renewal.

Help us, Parent of all parents, to care for ourselves
    properly and regularly,
    in body, mind, and spirit,
        so that we can be as present and effective as
            possible,
    and model the *shmirat hanefesh*/self-care we want our
        children to emulate.

May the words of Your prophet Malachi be fulfilled:
    "Behold, I will send you Elijah the prophet
before the coming of the great and terrible day of
    Adonai:
    And he shall turn the heart of the parents to the
        children,
    and the heart of the children to their parents."
    Amen.

A Prayer for Parents as They Accompany Their Child to Their First Day of School

Rabbi Daniel F. Polish

Ribbono shel olam, Av Harachamim, as a Father You have watched over me, protected me, and guided my footsteps. Now I, as a father, pray for my little child as I move him/her out of the sphere of my home out into the wider world. May his/her time at school be sweet for him/her. May his/her heart and mind open up with excitement to all the wonders he/she will meet as he/she begins his/her studies. May his/her classmates embrace him/her. May he/she know rich friendships that will span the years. But when disappointments come, as surely they will, *Ribbono shel olam,* may the tears he/she sheds water a plant of resilience within him/her. May he/she learn to rise up from his/her stumbles and grow from them. But above all, dear Father, may all the sweetness and openness and enthusiasm he/she has shown as a small child remain with him/her as he/she takes these first steps onto the path of his/her growing-up life.

Mother of Life

Rabbi James B. Rosenberg

Mother of life
Breast milk flowing ever fresh and free
You birth and rebirth our pulsing, blood bloom world
Newborn's cry, death's final rattle, spring rain's renewal
Young grass pushing through hard April earth
Your energy is ecstasy
You set the stars dancing in whirling constellations
Your breath vibrates reeds and strings to sing new songs.

Unto *Yah*!

Prayer for a Bar Mitzvah

Rabbi Hershel Jonah Matt

O God, I stand in the presence of the Torah, and in the presence of this congregation in Israel, on the Shabbat of my bar mitzvah.

Put the desire into my heart, O God, to love Your Torah and to study Your word which it contains—so that I may always learn from You: what to think, what to say, what to do.

Let me never forget that I am a Jew, a child of Your covenant, born into the community of Israel, which has been called by You to be a kingdom of priests and a holy nation.

Purify my heart, O God, and grant me strength of will, to serve You faithfully—so that I may ever act toward my fellow human beings in justice and in love. Thus will I bring joy to my dear ones, honor to the people Israel, and glory to Your holy name. Amen.

On the Process of Arranging Adoption
A Young Man's Prayer

Avinu shebashamayim, our Father who is in heaven,
At Sinai Moses received the Torah and handed it over
    to Joshua,
Who handed it over to the elders,
Who handed it over to the prophets,
Who handed it over to the men of the Great
    Assembly,
Who passed it down to us.
Let us not be the break in that chain of tradition.
Abraham had Isaac to re-dig his wells so that the water
continued to flow.
    Rebecca drew water from the well of loving-kindness so
    that she could join with Isaac.
    Together they used these waters to water the seed
        that would
    become Israel.
May we be blessed with children
So that we may draw from these same waters
And give them to these children
So that they may drink deeply from the traditions
And grow into strong shoots from the branches of Israel,
Your treasured people in whose praise You dwell.

*Baruch Atah Adonai, Eloheinu Melech Ha'olam, Moshivi
    akeret habayit, em habanim smeicha.*
Blessed are You, O Lord our God, King of the universe,
    who transforms a
barren woman into a happy mother of children.

On Losing a Fetus

Rabbi Lawrence Kushner (adapted)

Yehido shel olam, Holy One of Being,
Source of all life, Destiny of all souls,
receive the soul of this one that was
Not-Yet-A-Life-But-Only-A-Dream.
Send us healing in our grief and confusion.
Resilience through our loneliness and despair.
Give us strength to understand what has happened
and the ability to look for a future once again
filled with new life and new dreams.
Let hopeful parents everywhere,
who have endured the agony of decision and loss,
soon be comforted by the sounds
of an infant's cooing, crying, and laughing.

A Prayer of Comfort Following a Miscarriage

Rabbi Arnold Stiebel

O Heavenly Mother, Comforter of Your people, the One who shares sorrow with Your creation, be with us now as we experience the loss of potential life. We are sad as we think of the hopes for our unborn child, as in our minds we imagine what might have been.

Life is a fabric of different emotions and experiences. Now, while we experience life's bitterness and pain, be with us and sustain us. Give us peace and consolation. Help us to gather strength from within ourselves, from each other, and from our family and friends during this time of pain.

We pray that the soul of our unborn child, taken from us before its first breath, be restored to You. May it know Your presence, to feel and sense Your love for all eternity. May it once again be a spark in the radiance of Your existence.

Blessed are You, O Lord, God of compassion, who comforts the bereaved and shares sorrow with Your creation. Amen.

A Prayer for Fertility

Rabbi Craig Marantz

Please make my body fertile so that my lifeblood may
flow and my legacy may live in the life of a child I
have helped to create. Please support and calm me as
I seek this most precious blessing. Grant me patience
and forgiveness for myself and those I love as I search
for this elusive abundance. Help me, O God, to find
wholeness of body and spirit.

In Anticipation of IVF

Rabbi Allen Selis

We stand in awe of Your blessings, our God, for creating man and woman in Your image and blessing them with the power to create new life. Bless You, God, for creating human life.

An Insertion into the *Amidah* for Autism

Rabbi Bradley Shavit Artson

You graciously favor humans with discernment, and
   teach people
understanding. Grant us of Your discernment,
   understanding, and
insight.
May it be Your will, Adonai my God and God of my
   fathers and mothers,
that you swiftly send a heart discerning and wise, a
   refined tongue, and
true speech to my dear child, with whose soul my own is
bound. Grant strength, mercy, and compassion to us,
   to his family, and to
his teachers, as it is written: "Be strong and resolute; do
   not be terrified or
dismayed."
You are bountiful, Adonai, granting discernment.

As Partner / Spouse / Friend

A Prayer for Friendship

**Rabbi Elimelech of Lizhensk,
translated by Natan Ophir (Offenbacher)**

Protect and shield us from jealousy between a person
and his/her friend.

Let not jealousy enter our hearts and may others not be
jealous of us.

On the contrary, place in our hearts the ability to
see only the good in our friends, and not their
shortcomings!

May we instruct each other in the just and desirable
way before You.

And may there be no hate between friends.

From a Wedding Blessing

Rabbi James Stone Goodman

About God, bless You, O holy Maker of matches,
for the work of creation that You have taken up,
this tinker with the world.
Once creation was finished,
You turned to human beings in a different capacity.
We thank You for this obsessive preoccupation
since Genesis:

Making marriages.

Bless these two,
not-new,
a clever match,
nice work.

For a Wedding Anniversary

Rabbi Hershel Jonah Matt

We turn to You, O God, in gratitude for our married
love;
touch our heart, we pray with Your own.
Teach us to know that on this day and every day
we stand in Your very presence, fully exposed to
Your gaze.
Grant us faith and strength to remove all tarnish
from our love, renewing it as of old. Amen.

For a Wedding Anniversary

Rabbi Hershel Jonah Matt

Renew our love this day, O God.
Forgive us for profaning the holiness of love
whether by acts of cruelty done
or acts of tenderness left undone.
Purify our hearts,
that we may become ever sensitive
to each other's needs
and to Your will.

Blessing for Coming Out (in any and every way that calls for celebration)

Andrew Ramer (adapted from the original)

I praise You, Source of life, who said "*Lech lecha*" to Abraham and Sarah, our ancestors, "Go forth. Go find yourself." And they left their home, the only world they knew, to begin again in a new land, in a new way.

God of creation, who renews Your work each day, be with me now as I step out into the world in my own new way.

God of revelation, be with me as I affirm that I will move proudly through life as the strong loving wise beautiful person/people You made me/us to be.

God of redemption, in coming out today in community, I fulfill the command you gave to our ancestors. "*Lech lecha.* Go forth. Go find yourself." And so I have, for life and health, for joy and blessing. Amen.

Blessing for Someone in a Difficult Relationship

Andrew Ramer

Trouble runs in our family.
Abraham and Sarah walked out on theirs.
He didn't do well with either of his sons,
and then there's the sad story of
Hagar and Sarah's rivalry.
Esau and Jacob battled.
Rachel and Leah vied for Jacob's affection.
Their sons sold a brother into slavery,
tricked, lied, deceived, then killed.
And now God,
now that I find myself in a difficult relationship,
grant me patience, forgiveness, tolerance, strength,
and the ability to chart a clear course
through anger, sorrow, despair, and fear
to soulful clarity and compassion again
for both of us.

A Prayer for Being Single

Andrew Ramer

O God and God of all people, as first You created one human being, female and male in Your image, so do I stand before You now, one, complete and whole. Fully engaged in Your world, I open myself to You this day as did Miriam the Prophet, for whom Torah names no spouse, who served You all the days of her life, wholly and fulfilled. I come before You alone, like Elijah, who has traveled with our people since ancient times, blessing and watching over us. I am blessed and holy, sanctified and beloved. I am a singular witness and reflecting mirror of Your eternal Oneness.

As Son

A Psalm
In Memory of My Father

Rabbi Mike Comins

You God,
> before whom the flower bud in the meadow is about
> > to blossom with the rain or wither with the wind.

You God,
> before whom my father's dimentia stikes terror and
> > inspires love.

You God,
> before whom the delicious waves roll blue and froth
> > white, battering the rock in spectacular beauty or
> > smothering a village caught unawares.

You God,
> Creator. Destroyer.
> It's beautiful. It's cruel.
> It's all beautiful. It's all cruel.

So, my friends,
> pity me when I see the sun drop behind the ocean
> > through red-streaked clouds and the Milky Way
> > shines so bright that I must cry,

and envy me when I visit my father, whose stiff,
  emaciated legs are drawn into his chest like a
  fetus in the womb, whose eyes stare at me with so
  much fear and longing that I must cry.
Pity me. Envy me.
  For I am alive.

To You, God,
  I say, thank You, with joy and gratitude.
Before You, God,
  I am silent in Job's silence.
And I must cry.

In Memory of a Parent Who Was Hurtful

Rabbi Robert Saks

Dear God,

You know my heart. Indeed, You know me better than I know myself, so I turn to You before I rise for Kaddish

My emotions swirl as I say this prayer. The parent I remember was not kind to me. His/her death left me with a legacy of unhealed wounds, of anger and of dismay that a parent could hurt a child as I was hurt.

I do not want to pretend to love, or to grief that I do not feel, but I do want to do what is right as a Jew and as a child.

Help me, O God, to subdue my bitter emotions that do me no good, and to find that place in myself where happier memories may lie hidden, and where grief for all that could have been, all that should have been, may be calmed by forgiveness, or at least soothed by the passage of time.

I pray that You, who raise up slaves to freedom, will liberate me from the oppression of my hurt and anger, and that You will lead me from this desert to Your holy place.

A Prayer for Aging Parents

Rabbi Arthur Segal

Dear God, my Heavenly Parent,
It has been taught that it takes three to create a human
life, a mother, a father, and You. You provide my soul,
and my human parents everything else. My father has
nurtured me when I was unable to do anything for
myself. I am certain there were times when he was very
frustrated. But You placed inside human parents an
innate love for their children so they could overcome
this natural frustration and nurture us. Now it is my
turn as a grown child to nurture my elderly parents.
You have taught me to honor my parents. Show me
each day, many times a day when needed, the way to
help my parents. Help me understand their needs and
provide them for them. Keep me from frustration and
anger. Keep me ever reminded of how my father and
my mother unselfishly gave me life, and the countless
hours and days they put aside their needs to attend to
mine. Help me love You, dear God, and by doing so,
love my parents, so that their last years on this earth
can be the best for them, understanding that I cannot
change them, but only love them as they wish to be.
May it be Your will. Thank You. Amen.

As Provider

On Unemployment

Rabbi Howard Cooper

No encounter in our lives lacks hidden significance:
whatever the frustrations we face, there are
opportunities for doing Your work at every moment
of our lives. Our daily acts of kindness, of generosity
and care, bring You into the world. This too is work,
avodah, the service of God. The work of redemption is
never complete. It is our task amidst the vicissitudes
of life, woven into our days, while our search for
employment goes on.

Upon Being Under- or Unemployed

Rabbi Joseph B. Meszler

"Out of the depths I call to You, God."
I have become unsure of myself,
afraid and—I admit—embarrassed,
not wanting to face those I love,
to explain and explain and explain.
I fear bills I cannot pay,
obligations I cannot meet,
painful changes in my loved ones' lives,
and promises I cannot keep.
How long will this go on?

Help me still give to those I love.
I know, God, my worth comes
not from the work I have
but from who I am.
Give me patience, strength, and courage
to accept help I do not want,
to reach out to others
when I would rather be independent.
Let me feel faith in my future.
And when—and I must say when—
I am more secure,
let me not forget gratitude
for having come through this hard time.

Prayer on Receiving Difficult News

Rabbi Daniel F. Polish

O God whose embrace left my father Jacob lame
O God who said to Moses, "No one can see My face …"
O God who said to Job, "Who are you to understand
   My ways?"

I have just received news that crushes my spirit and
robs me of speech. With what words can I approach
You? I cannot give thanks. I cannot ask to understand
what has befallen me. I cannot plead with You to
understand Your ways. At most I can ask You for
strength to bear this and calm to navigate myself
beyond these tides. No more. As for "prayer," my soul
resonates with Job, in this time of travail: "Though …
[You] slay me yet will I worship … [You]." Let these
ancient words be mine.

Prayer for a Man Struggling with Job Loss

Rabbi Daniel F. Polish

O God who commanded my ancestor Adam, "By the sweat of your face shall you eat your bread," for years I have earned my bread, supported my family, found meaning and even identity in my work. But now that path has been foreclosed to me. Help me to be strong in the midst of this adversity. Enable me to feel of value even now that I depend on the generosity of others for my bread. Give me the ability to rise beyond shame and self-pity to find joy and meaning in the other realms of my life. Help me to be present to my family. Let me not fall into despair or the torpor of inertia. Bless me with strength to persevere as I search for new paths. May I succeed in reestablishing myself in the world of work. And help me to know, always, that my life can have meaning and value no matter how I earn my bread.

As Leader

Assumption of a Leadership Role

Rabbi Avi S. Olitzky

Master of the universe, grant me the humility of
   our teacher Moses and the courage of our father
   Abraham as I embark upon this journey.

Bless me with the guile of Jacob, the might of Joshua,
   the wisdom of Joseph, and the fear and compassion
   of Isaac.

As the many look to me for insight and guidance,
   guard my tongue from evil and make my lips fluid.

Let me be neither stifled nor stammered.

Grant me the nerve to judge, but protect me from the
   urge of being judgmental.

Abet me to leave my worries at the threshold as I enter
   my home, shielding my family from the angst of
   leadership.

And above all, thank You for blessing me with this
   challenge.

May my will bend to Your Will, on High, now and
   always, for You are the Supreme Leader.

A Prayer for the Teacher

Rabbi Daniel F. Polish

Lam'lamed Torah l'amo Yisrael b'ahavah. O God, who teaches Torah to Your people Israel in love, guide me as I presume to teach those who turn to me. May I approach my task with a whole heart. May my purpose be to impart true understanding and insight and not mere self-aggrandizement or empty authority. May the ideas I share be correct and the words I clothe them in be appropriate and efficacious. May I inspire in my students a true excitement, perhaps even a passion, for that which is so important, even central, to my life. Spare me from stating something false or evoking confusion. Arouse in me understanding and empathy for those I teach … the reminder that I once sat where they sit now, the recollection of how fallible our understanding is and how prone we are to forget. I, too, have misunderstood or lost the thread of my own studies. Let me not be impatient with those who sit before me now, sharing those same qualities. May I teach out of my love for my subject and of those who learn from me. And may the seeds I plant bear fruit in the minds and souls of my students, now or sometime in the future, whether I have the privilege of knowing about the harvest or not. May the discharge of the task itself be sufficient reward.

Candle Lighting

Rabbi Rami M. Shapiro

Darkness blankets me.
Comforting, perhaps a bit frightening.
It harbors both dreams and demons.
I tap it for solace. I delve it for options.
I flee it for fear that it mirrors that
which I wish so desperately to avoid: Me.
Yet I am here not to embrace the dark
but to kindle the light.
Not to close my eyes forever,
but to open them this once.
I dwell amidst the dark and bring forth light.
Soft, fragile, flickering light.
The only light I know. The only light I can bear.
I bring it, yet it isn't mine.
I kindle it, yet it isn't me.
I am the light bearer only.

Where the world is dark with illness,
let me kindle the light of healing.
Where the world is bleak with suffering,
let me kindle the light of caring.
Where the world is dimmed by lies,
let me kindle the light of truth.

I vow to be worthy of this honor
as I strike this match and kindle the flame that
     illumines the heart of all the world.

Blessed is the One beyond light and dark
by whose power I sanctify Life with the lighting of
     these candles.

Our Physical Lives

Physical Healing

A Prayer for Health

Rabbi Menachem Creditor

God, may my work feel redemptive even when an
ocean of need feels like it will pull me down.

May I feel supported when I feel alone in my work.

O God, remind me when I fail that I can learn, and
that my life is more than my work.

O God, remind me when I succeed that I can learn,
and that deep success requires the efforts of many.

May I remember that going home is a crucial part of
the dream.

God, help me to remember that I am one of the people
I am called by You to serve.

May I feel undivided as I transition from sphere to
sphere, a whole person within Your world.

A Jewish Prayer for Healing

Adapted in part by Rabbi Harry K. Danziger

Merciful God, we pray to You for the recovery of all who are facing illness or pain. We join our prayers with all who love them. Grant them renewed strength and courage. Strengthen in them the healing powers You have placed within us all. Guide the hearts and hands of those who are entrusted with their care. Help all of us who share the anxiety of this illness to be brave and hopeful. Inspire us with courage and faith. Grant Your blessings to all who call upon You.

Oh God, who blessed our ancestors Abraham, Isaac, and Jacob, Sarah, Rebecca, Leah, and Rachel, send Your blessings to all who are ill. Have mercy on them, and graciously restore their health and strength. Grant them a *r'fuah sh'leimah*, a complete recovery. May healing come speedily.

May the knowledge of Your love and ours give added hope to them and to their dear ones. May they find even greater strength because our prayers are linked to theirs. When pain and fatigue are my companions, let there be room in my heart for strength. When days and nights are filled with darkness, let the light of courage find its place. Help me to endure the suffering and dissolve the fear; renew within me the calm spirit of trust and peace.

Baruch atah Adonai, rofeh hacholim. We praise You, Eternal God, the Source of healing and health.

Based on Psalm 77
In Sickness and Health

Rabbi Harold M. Schulweis

When I cry my voice trembles with fear
When I call out it cracks with anger.

How can I greet the dawn with song
when darkness eclipses the rising sun?

To whom shall I turn
when the clouds of the present eclipse the rays of
tomorrow?

Turn me around to yesterday
that I may be consoled by its memories.

Were not the seas split asunder
did we not once walk together through the waters to
the dry side?

Did we not bless the
bread that came forth from the heavens?

Did Your voice not reach my ears
and direct my wanderings?

The waters, the lightning, the thunder
remind me of yesterday's triumphs.

Let the past offer proof of tomorrow
let it be my comforter and guarantor.

I have been here before
known the fright and found Your companionship.

I enter the sanctuary again
to await the echo of Your promise.

In Sickness and Health

Rabbi Harold M. Schulweis

> You who blessed our ancestors
> at the sea and in the desert
> bless these ill friends
> through us Your witnesses,
> Give us the wisdom to impart
> to them courage and hope.
> Let them know that they have
> in our holy community
> men, women, and children
> who pray for the skill of the physician
> who pray for their recovery
> of body and spirit.
>
> Teach us to remember Thy words
> out of the void and vastness of the darkness
> "Let there be light."

The Hurt

Danny Siegel

Whether the pain is real or not,
it is real for us.
Soothe us. Heal us.

Mental/Emotional Healing

An Unexpected Miracle

Rabbi Eliahu J. Klein (excerpted from original)

Let us see each and every moment of our life
as an unexpected miracle.
Let us not wait for catastrophes
to open our hearts to You, Creator of all healing.
Let us look at all moments as holding the possibility of
a miracle.
Sometimes a spontaneous prayer from the heart is a
miracle.
Sometimes listening to another person is a miracle.
Sometimes even a tear or a smile from a sad person is a
miracle.
Let the Creator of healing inspire us to see in many
moments
throughout the days of our lives
a possibility for the miraculous:
unexpected and intimate.

A Prayer of Healing for Mental Illness
Rabbi Elliot Kukla

May the One who blessed our ancestors bless all who live with mental illness, our caregivers, families, and friends. May we walk in the footsteps of Jacob, King Saul, Miriam, Hannah, and Naomi, who struggled with dark moods, hopelessness, isolation, and terrors but survived and led our people. Just as our father, Jacob, spent the night wrestling with an angel and prevailed, may all who live with mental illness be granted the endurance to wrestle with pain and prevail night upon night. Grace us with the faith to know that though, like Jacob, we may be wounded, shaped, and renamed by this struggle, still we will live on to continue an ever unfolding, unpredictable path toward healing. May we not be alone on this path but accompanied by our families, friends, caregivers, ancestors, and the Divine Presence. Surround us with loving-kindness, grace, and companionship, and spread over us a *sukkat shalom*, a shelter of peace and wholeness. And let us say: Amen.

Bodily Function and Formation

Asher Yatzar
Traditional Blessing of Bodily Function

Translation adapted from Rabbi Jeffrey Goldwasser

Blessed are You, Eternal our God, who formed the human body with wisdom and placed within it a miraculous combination of openings and organs. It is evident and known before Your honored throne, that if only one of them should be opened or blocked at the wrong time, it would be impossible to exist and stand before You. Blessed are You, Eternal One, the Healer of all flesh and Worker of wonders.

Asher Yatzar (The One Who Forms)
A Prayer of Gratitude for Our Bodies for Men, Women, Intersex, Transgender People, and Everybody Else

Rabbi Elliot Kukla

Baruch at Adonai Eloheinu Melech ha'olam asher yatzrah et ha'adam b'chochmah.

Blessed are You, Eternal One our God, Ruler of the universe, who has formed the human being with wisdom.

You created in the human body openings upon openings and cavities upon cavities. It is clear and well known that if just one of these unique valves within the complexity of each body were blocked or ruptured, it would be impossible to survive. May the day come when it is also obvious and evident that if just one unique body within the complexity of Your world is blocked or ruptured, if just one of us is not allowed to make our distinctive beauty manifest in the world, then it is impossible for all of Your creation to thrive and rise each day joyfully before You. Blessed are You, Source of all life and form, who implanted within us the ability to shape and reshape ourselves—molding, changing, transitioning, and adorning our bodies—so that the fullness of our many genders, the abundance of our desires, and the diversity of our souls can be revealed.

Blessed are You, Eternal One, who has made me Your partner in daily completing the task of my own formation.

My Body as Teacher

Rabbi James L. Mirel

Blessed are You, the Eternal One our God, Wondrous
Fashioner and Sustainer of Life, I thank You, God, for
giving me life. Help me to recognize my body as my
teacher. Help me to gracefully tolerate my limitations
and to grow in compassion through whatever pain I
might experience. Help me love myself, my body, as
one way of loving You. Help me use my mind and body
in the service of Your purpose in whatever ways are
possible today.

Pain as Teacher

Rabbi James L. Mirel

Blessed are You, the Eternal One, Source of all Life,
I awaken today with pain in my body. This pain is
part of living in this world. It reminds me of so many
people around the world who are also in pain. Despite
my illness or disability, I know You are with me. I pray
for strength and courage to live today to its fullest
in celebration of the spirit that You placed within
me. Please stay near me. You are my comfort and my
strength.

Medical Procedures

A Personal Prayer before a Doctor's Visit

Rabbi Jesse Olitzky

Adonai Tzuri, my Rock, my Redeemer, my Shield, and my Comfort, guard me and guide me. *Ribbono shel olam*, Master of the universe, and Creator of life, You have the wisdom to fashion the human body as a holy vessel. I marvel at the mystery of my body, the intricacies of organs and glands, and thank You for reaching this moment. I pray for good health, for sound mind, body, and soul. Protect me and sustain me. Please continue to watch over my soul, to watch over my self. I yearn for the strength and spirit to embrace any challenges I encounter in life's journey. Watch over and protect the nurses, physicians, caregivers, and all who take care of me, to, if need be, guide me back to full strength and good health.

May I always find comfort and security under the *kanfei HaShechinah*, protected by Your calming Divine Presence. I know that I will never need to search for You because You are always with me. Feeling Your presence, knowing Your presence, allows me to face my fears, conquer the unknown, and ensure a *refuat hanefesh*, a restored soul, as I pray for a *refuat haguf*, a healthy, pure, and whole self. For *Adonai li v'lo ira*, God, You are with me, and I shall not fear. Amen.

A Prayer for the First Time You Go through a Particular Moment of Vulnerability on the Physician's Table

Rabbi Jeffrey Salkin

Blessed are You, Adonai our God,
Who places within us holes and passageways,
Hollow places that are not yet hallowed places.*
Blessed is the healer's hand and the healer's eye
Who sees all the secret places within me
And reads them like a road map that will determine
   my destiny.
O God, who opens the gates of the decades of our lives,
I go through a passage as well.

---

* This plays on the Hebrew *chilulim*, "hollow places/passageways," and *chilul*, which means "that which is not holy."

Postoperative Prayer
In Sickness and Health

Rabbi Harold M. Schulweis

Early in the dawn
before the bustling of the carts
an old prayer
recited too quickly
now resonates anew.

For opening the eyes of the blind
For releasing the bound
For raising up the bowed down
For clothing the naked.

A prayer with new meaning
For clothing bent-over bodies
For straightening the spine
For guiding the steps of the faltering
For guiding the weak with resolve
For strengthening the weary.

May I not soon forget
lifted from gurney to bed
the free motion of a tubeless body
the first meal with teeth, tongue, and mouth.
May I not soon forget
the first lucidity
the first cessation of pain

the first walk without the arms of others
the sweet fatigue of the first shower.
May I not soon forget
the vigil of families
the wishes of friends
the donors of blood and prayer
the firm grip of doctors.
May I not soon forget
the day of leaving
the triumphant return
the turn of the lock
the loyalty of the mezuzah
standing watch, in good weather and bad.
To whom to give thanks
to whom is thanks not due
to the Source of healing
whose hands touch wounds
and voice encouragement
who feels with me
my doubts, my fright
my regrets,
my resolution.
May I not soon forget
the miracle
morning, noon, and night
the miracle within me and without.

Aging

God of My Body

Rabbi Joseph B. Meszler

God of my body,
too often I think only
of what I used to feel:
strength, effortless movement,
a boyhood memory of climbing a tree
or casually hopping a fence.
Now too often my body is a source of complaint.
I think of what hurts, what I can no longer do,
frustrated expecting what used to be.
What was once automatic and natural
now takes thought and attention.

Fashioner of flesh and bone,
help me remember
my body is still a miracle.
This skin, these senses
are the vehicle through which
I experience the world.

Let me be gentle with myself,
taking in the touch, smell, sight,
taste, and sound around me.
"The eye is never satisfied with seeing,
nor the ear filled with hearing."
Perhaps my unwelcome slowness is a lesson
in feeling the deep stretch, the full breath,
taking time to look at what is around me.
God, teach me to appreciate and accept
my body, Your vessel of wonder.

Ageless Aging

Rabbi Nachman of Breslov

Teach me, God,
to live out my days
focused on
all that is meaningful in life.
As unaccountable aches and pains
multiply,
as memory and retention
fade,
teach me to relate to my physical existence
with an ever-expanding recognition
of its transient nature;
teach me to relate to my soul
with an ever-expanding awareness
of her eternal nature
and ageless worth.

Psalm 22
Number My Days This Way

Danny Siegel

O Lord—
Number my days this way:

Days of strength to lie,
if the truth brings torment.
Days of weakness,
if strength gives rise to suffering.
Days of noise,
if silence is the cause of loneliness.
And
Nights of disconcerting dreams
if I turn smug to the taste of hunger.

Pursue me,
Discomfort me,
Destroy my own complacency
with paradox and contradiction.

Remind me I am Yours.

Community

Community

Danny Siegel

Do not heal *me*.
In the plural of our human selves
is relief and restoration.
Heal *all of us*,
and *I* will be healed.

On the Threshold of the Sixth Day

Hillel Zeitlin, translated by Joel Rosenberg

On the occasion of my fiftieth birthday, in the month
  of Sivan (May–June), 5681 (1921)

Fifty years I have lived in Your presence, fifty years of
  the "week" of my life—five decades
  of the seventy years of the typical human life.
On the threshold of the sixth day, I walk before You—
  the threshold of the sixth decade of
  life. On the threshold of the Sabbath eve of my life's
    days.
Give me the strength to run before You, on this, my
  Sabbath eve, that I might stand before
  You upon my Shabbat.
Give me a Youthful vitality, a firmness of character and
  holiness of will, to repair on this,
  my Sabbath eve, the sins of my earlier days.
For truly, I've blemished the root of my soul, I've
  damaged the channels, I've sealed off the
  wells, I've rejected divine abundance.
For truly, without knowing, I touched holy worlds up
  above and cut down Eternity's
  plants.
For truly, I've distanced myself from Your presence, like
  all who pass through this vale of
  tears.

For I've grown far away from You, yet You haven't
   gone far from me.

For I've gone astray, and You have always looked for me.

For I've gone astray, like a sheep that is lost, and You
   called me suddenly and I heard.

For You called to me and I turned to You, and I was
   able to come back to You.

I walked after You, but my knees often stumbled, from
   walking too much in alien fields.

For truly, I walked after You even while straying, in
   days I spent hiding and in days of
   the strength of my Youth.

For truly I've grown weary with the toil of my life, and
   You haven't yet shown me Your
   good, You haven't yet shown me Your ways.

But I truly continue to walk after You, and I stumble
   and rise, I stumble and rise …

When will You lift me, my Creator, so that I shall not
   stumble any more?

For truly, I've found You. But why do You hide?

For truly, I've found You, but I, to my woe, suddenly
   push You away.

For truly, I've found You, but why does my flesh not
   crave Your holy fire?

For truly, I've found You, but why are there hungers
   and yearnings still in me that aren't
   a desire for You?

Whom else do I have, in heaven or in earth, but You?
   Why do I still wander and stumble?
For see, when I fled from Your face, You would seek
   me, but now that I seek You, You're
   like one who flees me!
Have I truly fled from Your face before now? I *imagined*
   I was fleeing Your presence. But
   can one escape from God?
Can one escape from God's soul of all souls, from
   divinity's life of all lives?
But You have established a mystery in You, whereas I
   had imagined You'd grown distant
   from me and I had grown distant from You.
And You have numbered all the moments of my life.
   You have made known to me, God,
   what You have made known.
You have allowed me to fall into a Sheol of despair,
   that I might come out and bring others
   from there. You have allowed me to taste the taste
    of death, the taste of doubt
   without end, in order to live and enable others to live.
You've allowed me to fall in the depths of the ocean,
   so that my pain might grow, so my
   cry might grow louder, so my yearning for You might
    grow stronger.
You've allowed me to fall into pits of uncleanness, so
   I'd know and be warned, and give
   warning to my brethren.

Is such what You've done for me? Why have You left
   me to my soul?
You who know my sitting and my rising, don't You yet
   know that my feet are sometimes
      liable to fail?
For like the thunderbolt that cracks before my eyes,
   Your light may sometimes disappear,
And I'm left alone with myself, amid a darkness
   immense, until I multiply my cries to You,
      from the midst of the dark where I dwell.
If You have done thus to me, if You have cast me into
   Sheol, so that I might arise, and bring
      many up with me,
if I fulfill Your will, and enact Your word,
then pour out Your light on me, fill with it all that's
   within me.
As I enter a day of great toil, let me, I pray, carry out
   Your command that has called me
      from the depths of Sheol.
Let Your spirit rest on me. Let Your counsel make me
   wise. Let Your will be my will.

Grief

Comfort by God

Psalm 23

Translated by Rabbi Kerry M. Olitzky

Adonai is my Shepherd; I lack nothing

You give me my ease in fertile pastures

  You lead me to drink in tranquil waters

  You renew my soul

  You guide me on straight paths as befits Your
    reputation.

Even though I walk through the valley of the deepest
  darkness,

I will fear no evil

  For You are [always] with me.

Your comforting rod provides me solace.

You prepare a table for me [to eat at ease] in front of
   my enemies;
   My head oozes with oil; my cup is overflowing.
Surely merciful goodness will be mine throughout my
   life,
   And I will always remain in Adonai's precinct.

Inspired by Psalm 30:12–13

Rabbi Avi S. Olitzky

You upended my lament into dancing, You removed me from my mourning clothes and dressed me with happiness. As such, all that is glorious in this world will unceasingly sing praise to You; I will give thanks to You, Adonai my God, forever.

A *Yizkor* Blessing

Rabbi Bradley Shavit Artson

Blessed is the One who created you in judgment, who
   brought death to you
in judgment, and who will raise you up in judgment.

PESIKTA RABBATI, PISKA 12:1

God, Your love shines in the wise judgment to create
us—finite and precious—aware at each moment and
especially at this sacred moment, that our time is
limited, that we will each join our mothers and fathers
who have gone the way of all the earth, that we are
eternally dying and learning thereby to live.

God, Your firm judgment imposes upon us the
awareness of dying, which spurs us to live our lives in
desperate appreciation, numbering and living each day
to the full, illumined and inspired by the memories of
our dear ones who have already offered up their lives to
the eternal renewal of life itself, and of the cosmos.

Their memory and love raise us up in this world, as
better people, as more caring and more courageous
than we would have been without their deeds of love.
We are embraced and fortified by their continuing
impact in our hearts and our actions.

We gather, strong in memory and faith, affirming that You, God, will raise up our lives in this world, and one day will raise us up to them, all of us embraced by a love eternal, persistent, and redeeming. And let us say: Amen.

Prayer for a Mourner

Rabbi Bradley Shavit Artson

Your love shines in the wise judgment to create us—finite and precious—aware at each moment and especially at this sacred moment, that our time is limited, that we will each join our mothers and fathers who have gone the way of all the earth, that we are eternally dying and learning thereby to live.

Your firm judgment imposes upon us the awareness of dying, which spurs us to live our lives in desperate appreciation, numbering and living each day to the full, illumined and inspired by the memories of our dear ones who have already offered up their lives to the eternal renewal of life itself, and of the cosmos.

Their memory and love raises us up in this world, as better people, as more caring and more courageous than we would have been without their deeds of love. We are embraced and fortified by their continuing impact in our hearts and our actions.

We gather, strong in memory and faith, affirming that You will raise up our lives in this world, and one day will raise us up to them, all of us embraced by a love eternal, persistent, and redeeming.

Our Children

Rabbi Robert Scheinberg (adapted from the original)

From the mouths of young children
may You establish Your power
against Your enemies,
to silence every foe and avenger.

> PSALM 8:3

Our children are our guarantors.

> SHIR HASHIRIM RABBAH 1:4

Our hearts break any time we hear of violence
afflicting the innocent—all the more so when we
hear of the tragic loss of children.

Dear God, be with the parents, siblings, and other
family members who are mourning an unthinkable
tragedy today; send them comfort, light, strength,
and peace.

Help us to create a world where all children can be safe
to grow up and thrive,
where we can promise our children that their worst
nightmares will never be real.

Help us to create a world where troubled people can
readily find the solace they seek

and can never achieve the power to inflict their
torments on others.

Our children are our guarantors. May we be worthy to
be their protectors.

El Malei Rachamim for Parents

God filled with mercy,
dwelling in the heavens' heights,
bring proper rest
beneath the wings of your *Shekhinah*,
amid the ranks of the holy and the pure,
illuminating like the brilliance of the skies
the souls of our beloved and our blameless parents
who went to their eternal place of rest.
May you who are the source of mercy
shelter them beneath your wings eternally,
and bind their souls among the living,
that they may rest in peace.
And let us say: Amen

Prayer upon the Death of a Parent

Andrew Meit (adapted from the original)

God, please do kiss warmly my mother/father hello
as we struggle to kiss her/him good-bye.

God, please favor me, to inhale smoothly her/him into
Your heart
as we exhale our rough grief from our entangled hearts.

God, please with grace, lift quickly and wholly her/him
into Your embrace
as we endure slowly her/him leaving this world's firm
grip.

God, please grant me for You to slide quickly her/his
body from her/his meritorious soul,
a soul providing sustaining milk/support to many for
many years in many ways.

God, please with compassion place her/his soul among
her/his loved ones and friends
as we place her/his body among beloved flowers and
fertile earth.

God, please always show and remind me the many,
blessed memories of her/him
till the day I too die,

Amen.

Praying for What Is Lost

Rabbi David Wolpe

Dear God, how do we pray for what was lost? We cannot pray for deliverance or a miracle, for the tragedy has already burned itself into our souls. Children have grown fatherless. Families are long since bereaved. We know there is no prayer to change the past.

So we pray to live with memory, with constant love, with the promise both to combat evil and to cherish goodness. Do not let our pain cloud our hopes or crush our hearts. Help us grow through this tragedy, keep faith with its victims, and sustain our trust in You.

The Gate of Tears

Hillel Zeitlin, translated by Joel Rosenberg

Day and night, I cry out before You,
day and night, I cry out before You,
and there is none to answer.
My inmost depths cry out to You,
and there is none to answer.
The hidden pinpoint of my soul is yearning for You,
but there is none to answer.

While once, in days of old, when I would seek You,
in my weeping, and cry out to You,
it seemed that Your support was clear to me.
But now, great walls divide us, me from You,
like gates of iron bolted shut,
and yet, by the tradition of Your holy teachers, You
have declared:
"All gates are closed up but the Gate of Tears."
    (Babylonian Talmud, *Berakhot* 32b)
But now even these gates are closed and locked.
There's none to open them!
"Hope for THE ETERNAL ONE! Your heart be strong
    and full of courage!" (Psalm 27:14)
"If you have prayed but not been answered, pray once
    more!" (Babylonian Talmud, *Berakhot* 32b)

Until my final breath of life, I shall not cease from
     pouring out my thoughts to You,
My final breath of life shall be but song and prayer!
My final breath of life, caressing of Your spirit!
My final breath of life—a droplet in the ocean, a wisp
     of wind, a ray of sunshine—
     it shall be a breathing of the breath of Your Eternity.
White dove comes to rest upon my windowsill—and
     O, may it bring news of Your
     redemption!
A light wind blows upon my face—and O, may it bring
     me Your greeting!
A surge of light breaks forth into my room—and O,
     may it reveal a vision of Your
     consolation!

For Family Members

On the Death of a Father

By a young man whose father had recently died

I pray that you give my mother strength and peace. I thank you for blessing me with a father who was kind, loving, funny, and warm. I pray that I will always remember my father as he was when he was living.

Memorial Prayer for a Beloved Pet

Andrew Ramer

Source of life, you gave to Adam the task of naming all the animals, and at times, in the midst of your teeming world, we live so closely with them that we give ourselves their names, and in a way we become them: Dov—bear, Rachel—ewe, Deborah—bee, Zev— wolf, Tzvi—deer, Zipporah—bird.

And now, one who has been dear to me is gone from this world—my beloved companion, close to my heart and named by me, who spoke to my soul in a language of its own—who brought tenderness, warmth, joy, and healing to my life.

Source of the breath of all flesh, hold me in my loss, and comfort me as I move though the world in sorrow, and return home to a silence that makes my heart weep, so that I forget my own name.

Suffering

This Is My Prayer

Hillel Bavli (adapted)

Translated by Norman Tarnor

This is my prayer to You, my God:
Let me not swerve from my life's path,
Let not my spirit wither and shrivel
In its thirst for You
And lose the dew
With which You sprinkled it
When I was young.

May my heart be open
To every broken soul,
To an orphaned life,
To every stumbler
Wandering unknown
And groping in the shadow.

Bless my eyes, purify me to see
Humanity's beauty rise in the world.

Deepen and broaden my senses
To absorb a fresh
Green flowering world,
To take it from it the secret
Of blossoming in silence.

Grant strength to yield fine fruits,
Quintessence of my life,
Steeped in my very being
without expectation or reward.

And when my time comes—
Let me slip into the night
Demanding nothing, God, of humanity
Or of You.

Take Off My Heavy Burden

Rabbi Shlomo Carlebach

Merciful, unburden me, deliver me. Please don't wait any longer.

O Lord

Rabbi Adam D. Fisher

O Lord, You come astride the wind,
wrapping Yourself in the dawn.
You ride a chariot drawn by a hundred horses
galloping, hurling near
then rein them in,
step off in soft air
to embrace me,
pull me up to fly over hills
past the tire and sneaker prints on the beach
a Budweiser can, deposit uncollected,
Mars bar wrappers,
leavings of wind and moon;
past the grave of a 16-year-old girl—
died when thrown through the window
of an overturned car skidding on its roof,
mourned for her—could have been my daughter;
fly through hills,
sun low and golden across the grass:
breathe the calm,
see teenage girls run across the road,
skip in delightful freedom;
fly to my newly tilled garden
where I walk in spongy soil—
the world's soft breast,

where dew forms pearls
in green nasturtium leaves,
where the trowel enters
soft, moist soil,
clunks against small stones,
cuts a web of old roots,
pushes past a rolled-up grub
and makes space for baby's breath;
where I dig a hole to plant a white pine,
fill it with water,
see a beetle struggle.
I try to imagine its terror,
attempt to lift it out
with my shovel.
I fail. It drowns.
I ride the quick current
carrying me down,
like a yellow leaf
blown in the stream,
float past rocks,
am caught on twigs,
swirl in whirlpools,
afraid the wrong move,
will make me drown.
O Lord, ...

The Meaning of Suffering

Rabbi Levi Yitzchak of Berditchev

Eternal Presence of the world, I am not asking You
to show me the secret of Your ways,
for it would be too much for me.
But I am asking You to show me one thing:
what is the meaning of the suffering
that I am presently enduring,
what this suffering requires of me,
and what You are communicating to me through it,
Eternal Presence of the world.
I want to know
not so much why I am suffering
but whether I am doing so for Your sake.

A Poem Addressed to You

Rabbi James B. Rosenberg

Adonai natan, v'Adonai lakach ...
"Adonai has given,
and Adonai has taken away ..."

JOB 1:21

Oh, the day that Edith, eyes blank as snow,
Hooted broken bird-song sounds
That snapped forever the twisted cord
Binding mother to son:
Who-are-you?

Where were You
When my father phoned me on his long night of
    hopelessness?
She thinks I'm an impostor. What can I do?
How language hangs helpless. Mother drowning
In a sea of words. What can I do?
What can I do?

Were You with me in the nursing home?
Were You there? Mother undressing, garment by
    garment,
Crazy cacophony of ancient eating sounds
Sucking me into a black hole of helpless humiliation.

Mother spilling sentence fragments
Like pieces of an unsolved jigsaw.
Mother, let me stay a half an hour more,
Let me put your life together again,
Piece by piece.

Hear the rain-damp clumps of April clay
Thump-thumping on the casket,
Ghost sounds linking past and future.
Flowing teenage tears, my son's tears—
I command him with my eyes:
One day, David, you will do this for me,
Shovelful by shovelful.

O Devouring Presence,
You have taken away, and You have given back again.
Open now the graves of memory and of hope
And breathe Your Weary Self into these weary bones!

Communal Prayers

Communal Prayer of Remembrance

O God, remember today those members of our family who were martyred in years past because of their sexual or gender identity: those murdered by fanatics in the Middle Ages, those who perished in the Holocaust, and those struck down in our own cities, in our own time. Remember also those who took their own lives, driven to despair by a world that hated them. And in mercy remember those who lived lives of loneliness, repressing their true nature and refraining from sharing their love with one another. O God, watch over the souls of these beloved ones: lesbian, gay, bisexual, transgender, and help us bring an end to hate and oppression of every kind.

The Hour of Remembrance

Rabbi Morley T. Feinstein

O God, Source of life, bestow Your loving-kindness on
all Your children at this hour of memory. Let us recall
our loved ones with candor and love, and inspire us
to gain strength from the flame of their memories to
kindle a beacon of hope for our future. Draw us near
to one another, that we might comfort each other, feel
the pain that unites us, and be more sensitive to those
around us. May we always praise You who, despite the
mystery of death, gives us the very life we cherish.

Gathering

Rabbi Rami M. Shapiro

We gather at this moment at life's most critical juncture. We gather upon ground hallowed by human longing, questioning, and fear. We gather at the edge of oblivion and cry out, straining with all our might to hear even the faintest of echoes rebound and return. We gather before the angel of death and demand to see its eyes, to look into its soul that we might know why all things must end.

But the angel's name is Silence, and darkness mocks our most feverish pleadings. Yet the lamp of life needs darkness to shine, just as the newborn's cry needs silence to be heard. If we would value the light, we must tap the darkness; if we would cherish the cry, we must pierce the Silence. One who dares stand in darkness can perceive what is in the light; but one who stands only in light cannot pierce the surrounding darkness.

There are no timely deaths, though some are more accepted than others.
There are no blessed deaths, though some are more peace-giving than others.

There are only unwanted deaths, uncontrolled,
   unreasonable, unholy deaths.
Death tears at the marrow of the living, shattering our
   facade of wisdom,
evoking the horror and the agony of our own
   transience.
Yet even as we peer into the heart of death and behold
   no answers,
a courage arises within us to face the truth of our
   ignorance with the light of our love.
Though we cannot know the reasons for death, we can
   face the reality of it with the best of human dignity;
   refusing to despair of life, even as life seems to have
   despaired of us.
Blessed is one with the power to listen to the Silence
   and to endure.

Protection

On Waking

Kavanah on Waking Up

Rabbi Andrew Shaw

In these still, quiet moments,
I am not asleep,
and not yet awake.

In the threshold of day and night,
with the mixture of darkness and light,
my body is once again coming to life.

I am reborn, each day,
from the womb of Your compassion.
May all of my actions
be worthy of the faith You've placed in me.
With words of thanks I'll greet the dawn.

230

Traveler

A Traveler's Prayer

May it be Your will, Adonai our God and God of our ancestors, to guide us to peace, directing our steps and sustaining us in peace, so that we may reach our destination in life in joy and in peace. Save us from our enemies, hidden foes, and disasters on our journey. Protect us from the evils that threaten our world. Send Your blessings upon whatever we do, and may we find grace, kindness, and mercy in Your eyes and in the eyes of all who look upon us. The God who hears prayers and supplications will listen to our pleas. Praised are You, Adonai, who hears our prayers.

A Prayer for Travel

Rabbi Menachem Creditor

Yehi ratzon milfanekha—May it be Your will,

Eternal One, God of our ancestors, that we journey toward peace, that our footsteps be guided toward peace, and that we reach our desired destinations for life, gladness, and peace. May we be protected from every obstacle along the way, and from all manner of challenge the world endures. May there be blessing in the works of our hands, and may we be granted peace, kindness, and mercy in the eyes of all who see us. May our prayer be heard, for You are the One who hears and holds all prayer. *Barukh atah Adonai, shomei'a tefillah.* Blessed are You, Eternal One, who hears prayer.

A Prayer for the Traveler

Rabbi Daniel F. Polish

O God, Guide of the roads of life, may the journey
upon which I am about to embark reward me with
new experiences, new vistas, and new opportunities
for growth. May my eyes see sights unseen before and
unanticipated. May my ears hear new melodies. May
my tongue resonate to new tastes. May I experience
joy and wonder. May I be introduced to people who
inspire in me a renewed reverence for the diversity of
the human family, people of wisdom who give me the
gift of new insights, perhaps even people who become
valued friends on the journey of life. May I encounter
challenges but incur no injury, sustain no illness,
or cause harm to others. In my travels may I be an
emissary of goodwill and understanding. And may it
be my privilege to be returned to my own home whole
and well.

Supplications

After Psalm 16
Rabbi Daniel S. Alexander

God, remind me that I need protection … when I forget.
And when pain or fear rise within me,
be there to embrace me,
to calm my shaken nerves,
to support my wobbly bones.

Remind me, You who drop hints in all the obvious
   places,
that Your hand enfolds my fate
as Your grace allows my portion.

Keep me in mind of the unending blessings showered
   upon me,
that I may take joy in them,
that I may express appreciation for them.

I thank You, God, for the guidance of wise mentors,
empathetic listeners, caring models of the way,
and for the knowing heart, the urgent bladder,
insistent peristalsis.

Do not abandon me to dread of night.
Do not release my hand
in the hour of my anguish.

Hold me even in my dying
for at the end, I know,
there is none but You,
no comfort but Yours,
no trust but in You.

In You do I find fullness and truth.

Following the *Amidah*

Rabbi Alexandri

May it be Thy will, O Lord our God, to station us in an illumined corner and do not station us in a darkened corner, and let not our heart be sick nor our eyes darkened!

Tefillah
A Prayer

Bezalel Aloni

God, watch over us, please, like children
watch please and don't leave
give us light and the joy of youth
give us strength, more and more
watch over us, please, like children
watch please and don't leave
give us light and the joy of youth
and let us love too.

A Prayer

Wally "Velvel" Spiegler

Hear my prayer, O Lord, heed my plea for mercy.

In time of trouble I call You, for You will answer me.

When pain and illness are my companions, let there be
room in my heart for strength.

When the days and nights are filled with darkness, let
the light of courage find its place.

Help me endure the suffering and dissolve the fear;
renew within me the calm spirit of trust and peace.

We praise You, O God.

Give Me Strength

Eliezer Bugatin, translated by Rabbi Chaim Stern

O God
give me strength to forget
evils over and done,
history's falls and fouls,
yesterday's frozen hope.

And give me strength to keep watch
for fair weather after a stormy day,
incense of flowers
and quiet waves.

Give me strength to wait and time to hope:
until the last day
strength to keep watch and rejoice
as doves are hatched and babes are born,
as flowers bud and blossom
and visions break out and grow.
Give me strength,
O God.

Give Me Light
Based on Psalm 123:3

Rabbi Shlomo Carlebach

My world is dark with disappointment.
Give me Your light, Lord.

A Prayer following the Fifteen Morning Benedictions

Freely translated by Rabbi Ira Flax

May it be Your will, *Yah* (Adonai) my God and the God
   of my ancestors, to protect me this day and each day
from the insults of others and to maintain humility in
   myself.

Save me from random violence, from deceitful friends,
   and neighbors who seek evil.

Protect me from the misfortune and travails of daily
   life.

Shield me from the temptations that would ruin my
   health and destroy the love of my family.

Spare me from unjust judgments and unjust officials
   who are harsh and ruthless, whether or not they
   embrace Your covenant.

Soul Dialogue No. 5

Rabbi James Stone Goodman

Master of the universe,

I am alone with my shoes and still I cannot move.
One step and the world would cease to exist.

Let me know in some abstract non-abstract way
in my deepest being, my soul, that it is safe.

Let me be wise myself, trust wisdom,
let us be wise together.

Let my soul speak freely to my heart.
Let my mind take a vacation now and again,
vacate the space so my soul might take up residence.

I am carrying my soul with me wherever I go.
Ahead: a field, a small house, a mountain,
I unpack my bag, take out a sandwich, and make tea.

I reach in, I pull up my soul—
it is a mouth now, a quill, a stick, a light, an inner
    shining,

It has taken the shape of prayers
I am speaking to You, from You, the same voice.

Save me, my soul.
Pick me up and lay me down, carefully.

A Prayer for My Subconscious in Response to the Rebbe's Torah

Rabbi Elihu Gevirtz

O God, Source of all breath
Go with me as I sleep
As I slumber down into the depths of my subconscious
Lead me to my guardian angel
Who will fly with me to a river of joy
That spills into the sea
That becomes vapor
Then rain
Then river
Of dreams, love, and commitment
to *mitzvot* that walk me to You.

I Have No Fear

Rabbi Robert N. Levine

Mi shebeirach avoteinu m'kor habrachah l'imoteinu, may the One who blessed our fathers and blessed our mothers …

Once again, the prayer for health resonates throughout the congregation.

But, dear God, I don't feel sick. I feel lost. I feel alone.

Yes, there are people in my life, but we don't connect.

Living parallel lives my mate and I sit at the same table typing furiously into our phones, oblivious to each other's presence, each other's plight.

I worry so about my child who also seems lost, but does not want to be found, at least by me.

So I turn to You, not to solve my problem, but so I will no longer be alone. You have defined yourself as *Ehyeh-Asher-Ehyeh*, I will be what I will be, a presence always. That's what I need, dear God, to know You are here and that You won't let me sink, won't let my child sink.

Please talk to me, not with booming sound or imperial
    tone.
Your commanding presence I cannot sense; what I
    need is a divine friend who will communicate in
    that still small voice that assures me that tomorrow
    can be better, that I can do better. If I can connect
    to You, somehow, maybe someday soon, I can
    connect to them.
Talk to me, my Divine Friend.
Help me to know You are here.
Then I will know that what the *Adon Olam* teaches, in
    fact, is true:
God is with me, I have no fear.

Yotzer HaAdam (Creator of Humankind)

Jay Michaelson

What a conundrum are the shapes of man and woman!
Misbehaving, alluring, defying all sense.

Sitting on a train, a young man crosses his legs.
What follicle or cell, what arrangement of ligaments
is responsible for the arising of lust?
Which of the curves or lines or angles
throws all my education to the fire,
reduces me, captures me, turns me from angel to fool?
And, for that matter,
what magic of genetics, parentage, or divine caprice
inclines me this way instead of that,
to man instead of others,
and yet more specifically—so precise are our wants—
to this hairstyle, and, oh dear, certainly not that one,
oh, and what *is* he trying to do with those *glasses*?

All this is *hevel*, says the preacher, and striving after
    wind—
lustful nonsense, undignified and adolescent.
But then, who listens to preachers, anyway,
other than more preachers?
(My apologies, of course, to the clergy.)

Or—herewith my sage advice to the grooms—
Time passes. Gravity wins. Hair disappears where it is
    wanted,
appears where it is unwanted.
Lines creep up unseen, weight moves inexorably
    downward,
one learns to eat with less abandon, or else suffer the
    consequences.
Indeed, flesh misbehaves, Former of humans!
Can You blame us for lasers and plastics,
for interventions in Your strategies of planned
    obsolescence?

(Of course,
really the body behaves quite precisely:
entropy, the laws of nature,
all this is *exactly* how it should be.
What misbehaves is the faculty of want.
But when have we humans
ever seen fit
to complain about our dearest preferences?)

Yet if the earth creature drives us mad with its beauty
    or its lack,
then too we must celebrate the formations of man
for their capacity to glue ... adhere ... join.
Adam and Steve, Lilith and Eve—

what would these couplings be without the capacity of
    loins to intermingle,
or brain-commanding lusts to draw us one to the other?
Yes, these absurd enchantments of shoulder, breast,
    pelvis, leg
have caused us all much embarrassment.
But here we are, under a canopy
erected by their noble wills,
as much as by any choice of man;
we stand in a home made for heart, but constructed of
    body:
a gift of the shapes of sames, opposites,
    alls-of-the-above.
We sanctify love in a body of lust.

I pray thus:
Former, You have made us out of earth and water.
We breathe wind as You did,
and within us we kindle fire.
Your forms to us are wondrous,
such that only when we look into another's eyes
do we blur their boundaries
and melt.

The Pit

Rabbi James B. Rosenberg

Deep in the pit,
Ooze seeping
Through time-worn shoes
Already damp from sweating feet.
A six-inch centipede
Creeps out of dark slime—
Each twitching leg a silence,
Unseen mouth quivering, expecting …
No grip on smooth mud walls
For trembling fingers.

Or is this pit
The deep dark down nest
Of an enemy within
Who continues to pursue me
On many legs?

If only I could hear the echo
Of Your cry of absence
Calling me, calling me,
The echoing cry of Your absence,
The echoing cry …

Tachanun (Supplication)
Rabbi Zalman Schachter-Shalomi

My God!
my soul is Yours
my body is Your servant
take pity on what You have created;
my soul is Yours
and my body is Yours
God help us for Your sake.
We come to You
because we want to honor
Your reputation.
Help us in our moral struggle
for the sake of Your reputation;
because You are kind and compassionate.
Forgive us,
for there is so much
we need to be forgiven for.
Pardon us our Father,
our errors are so great;
forgive us our Royal Master
many are our mistakes.
Our God our parents' God
pardon our sins
erase our rebellions

let our failures not appear before You.
Mold our drives to serve Your purposes;
let our stubbornness be in Your service.
Refresh our conscience
to guard Your instructions.
Sensitize our hearts to love You
and to respect Your reputation
as Your Torah prescribes:
"And *Yah* Your God
will sensitize Your heart
and the hearts of Your children
so that Your love for Your God
will be wholehearted, inspired,
to make Your life meaningful."

Dear God.
I approach You
from the desire to serve You
and yet there is no tzaddik
who can do only good
and not fail in it.
Please help me with my moral life
so that in every way
my attitude will be balanced
and right.
To begin with,
help me to forgive anyone

who is frustrated and upset me
if they have sinned against me,
my body my possessions
my reputation anything of mine
but unintentionally or intentionally
whether they scheme to do it
or were unaware
whether it was in word or action
whether is was in thought
and the imagination
whether it was in this incarnation
or in any other
I completely forgive any God-wrestler;
let no one be punished on my account.

    My God and my parents' God
    may our prayer come before You
    do not turn Your attention
    from our pleading
    we don't want to be impudent
    we don't want to be stubborn
    and claim that we are righteous
and have not sinned.
Indeed our parents have sinned
and we have sinned.
Help us God not to fail You again
and what I hereby confess to You

I beg You,

that in Your great mercy

You erase my sins

but not by means

of suffering and illness.

May the words of my mouth and the meditation of my
    heart

be acceptable for You *Yah* my Rock and my Redeemer

I place my faith in You

I place my trust in You

I place my hope in You.

T'shuvah—Coming Back Around

Rabbi Zalman Schachter-Shalomi

A year has gone by,
I say with a sigh—
O Lord I did not progress.
Your Torah not learned,
Your *Mitzvot* not earned,
This I am forced to confess.

I undertake
This to remake
My life anew to fashion.
So help me, please,
From sin to cease
And only to You
Give my passion.

I seek Your light,
I need Your aid.
Without Your joy
I am afraid.
Heal me God
In body and in soul.

Please, good God,
Pour out Your blessing,
That in Your sight
We'll be progressing.
O Lord above,
Let us feel Your love
And perceive You,
    Our souls caressing.

May we not be
Disappointed
In waiting for ben David
Anointed.
With Your open hand,
Bless our Holy Land
And our leaders
Whom we have appointed.

The Jewish People

Got fun Avraham (God of Abraham)
Said before Havdalah

Rabbi Levi Yitzchak of Berditchev

God of Abraham, Isaac, and Jacob, protect your beloved
people Israel in your love from all hurt. As the beloved
holy Sabbath goes away, may the week, month, and year
come to us with perfect faith, with faith in the sages,
with love and attachment to good friends, to attachment
to the blessed Creator, with belief in your thirteen
principles of faith, and in the ultimate redemption, may
it be soon, and the resurrection of the dead, and in the
prophecy of Moses, our teacher, may he rest in peace.

Lord of the world! You are the one who gives strength
to the weak! Give your beloved Israelites more health
and strength so we can love You and serve You, only
You, and no other, heaven forbid. And the week, and
the month, and the year should come to us with mercy,
health, auspiciousness, blessing, success, riches, and
glory, and to children, long life, abundant food, and
divine providence, for us and all for all Israel, and let
us say: Amen.

The Needs of Your People

Rabbi Hershel Jonah Matt

The needs of Your people, O God, are many;
Their own resources fall short.
May it be Your will to grant to each of us
What seems to be our need,
What seems to be our lack.
But, what is good in Your own eyes—this do.

How Many Miracles

Rabbi Hershel Jonah Matt

How many are the miracles
That You, O God,
Have wrought on our behalf,
Through all the ages
Since You first delivered us from Egyptian bondage—
When the sea was split
And we escaped from the pursuing foe.

If enemies arise again,
Deliver us again.

Humanity

A Prayer for People Living in Hunger around the World

Rabbi Shai Held

Avinu shebashamayim: On this and every day remember Your children, created in Your image, who hunger for bread and thirst for water. Take heed of all those who wander in search of food, whose worlds have gone dark through no fault of their own.

We lift up our hands to You for the lives of the myriad children who faint from hunger. Show them mercy and kindness, God, and do not abandon them in their time of despair. Please, Lord, do not let the righteous want for food.

Because You, Lord, provide the world with a bounty of food, while we have failed in our responsibility. We have stopped up our ears from the cries of the poor.

Open our eyes, Lord, so that we see the suffering of the poor; open our ears so that we hear their cries. Remove the calluses from our hearts so that we may pursue the *mitzvah* of *tzedakah* more carefully than all others; instill wisdom and courage within us so that we may empower those living in poverty. Strengthen their hands so that they not be dependent on the gifts or loans of other people, but only on Your full, open, brimming, and generous hand.

Oh God, speedily bring an end to poverty, so that "[the poor] shall not hunger or thirst, hot wind and sun shall not strike them, for Your mercy will guide them to springs of water." Fulfill Your promise to those who revere You, as it is written: "God will wipe the tears away from every face." Then shall we praise You, saying: "God has satisfied the thirsty, filled those who were hungry with all good things."

Amen, and so may it be Your will.

We Cannot Merely Pray to You

Rabbi Jack Riemer

We cannot merely pray to you, O God, to end war;
For we know that You have made the world in a way
That man must find his own path to peace.
Within himself and with his neighbor.

We cannot merely pray to You, O God, to end
    starvation;
For You have already given us the resources
With which to feed the entire world,
If we would only use them wisely.

We cannot merely pray to You, O God, to root out
    prejudice;
For You have already given us eyes
With which to see the good in all men,
If we would only use them rightly.

We cannot merely pray to You, O God, to end despair,
For You have already given us the power
To clear away slums and to give hope,
If we would only use our power justly.

We cannot merely pray to You, O God, to end disease;
For You have already given us great minds
With which to search out cures and healing,
If we would only use them constructively.

Therefore we pray to You instead, O God,
For strength, determination, and willpower,
To do instead of just pray,
To become instead of merely to wish.
That our world may be safe,
And that our lives may be blessed.

In the Armed Forces

A Prayer for Those in the Armed Forces
Rabbi Albert Ringer (adapted)

Our God and God of our Fathers and Mothers, today I
stand before You, knowing that I bring myself into
danger. Like Jacob asked You for support against
Esau, I ask You to help both me and my fellow
soldiers.

Please, be our shield, protect our ways, help us to make
our mission successful.

May it be Your will that no harm comes over us. May
it be Your will that we can return to this place in
peace, sound of body and whole of mind.

"Be the shield of my protection.

Let Your right hand support me.

Let Your word strengthen me."

Those who know Your name trust in You,

For You do not abandon those who turn to You,
Eternal One.

Blessed are You, Eternal One, who hears our prayer.

Gratitude

The Word Most Precious

Rabbi Abraham Joshua Heschel, translated and adapted by Rabbi Zalman Schachter-Shalomi

Each single moment greets my life,
A message clear from timelessness.
All names and words recall to me
The word most precious: God!

Pebbles twinkle up like stars,
Silent raindrops echo true,
What all creation echoes too,
My Father, Teacher, word from You.

My All, Your Name is my safe refuge.
Without Your nearness I am naught,
So lonely, saddening, is that thought.

All I possess, is just this word—
If forgetfulness would snatch a name from me
Let it be mine not Thine,
So screams in dread that heart of mine.

With every word I nickname You,
I call you "Woods" and "Night" and "Ah" and "Yes,"
With all my instants weaving sacred time
A bit of ever-always is my gift to You.

Would that for Eternity
I could celebrate a holiday for You.
Not just a day—a lifetime. Please!
How insignificant my thrift and gift

Of offerings and adoration.
What can my efforts do for You
But this: to wander everywhere and bear
a living witness that shows I care.

Hoda-a (Thanksgiving)

Rabbi Cary Kozberg

Praise to You for Mind—
Simple, fresh, confused, discerning.
Praise to You for thoughts
Appearing from nowhere,
Erupting out of dormant and unexplored spaces
Like flowing lava
Heating my will to create.

Praise to You for Soul—
Proud, humble, angry, naïve.
Praise to You for feelings that overwhelm
Yet give perspective:
Emotions unabashedly released,
Unashamedly realized,
Like a spring unfiltered through Intellect
Watering my will to live.

Praise to You whose image seeks true reflection.

In Thanks

Rebbe Nachman of Breslov

My God,
It has taken me time,
but I am finally learning
to trust You.
When I called, You answered;
when I cried; You sent relief;
when I was in need,
You came through.
You are there for me
in every instance.
I need only
look, think, and understand,
and I can always find You;
there you are,
always ready to help.
Thank You, God,
for waiting for me.

Recognizing Life's Miracles

Rabbi Nachman of Breslov

Open my eyes,
O God,
to the marvels that surround me.
Show me the wonder
of each breath I take,
of every
thought,
word
and movement.
Let me experience the miracles
of the world I witness—
ever mindful
and always appreciative
of all that You have made.

Some of the Things We Are Thankful for Today

Rabbi Jack Riemer

Let us thank God
For the many things we enjoy that cost nothing,
And that are worth everything.
Let us thank God for the joy of having grandchildren,
For we did not realize that they could make our lives so
   delicious.
Let us thank God for the teachers we had in our youth,
The ones who believed in us more than we believed in
   ourselves,
And who encouraged us to think, and then to think
   again.
Let us thank God for those rare souls
Who lifted us up when we were laid low by trouble,
And who would not let us give up.
Let us thank God for the people who light up our lives
   today
By their simple acts of *menschlichkeit*.
Let us thank God for the kindness of strangers,
At bus stops and in the supermarket
Who take the time to give us directions, and do not
   expect thanks.
Let us thank God for Beethoven's quartets,

And for Shakespeare's sonnets,

And for Rembrandt's portraits.

And let us thank God for the first cup of coffee in the
   morning,

For James Earl Jones's incredible voice,

And for Jerry Seinfeld's humor, and for Kramer's too.

Let us thank God for ballpoint pens, and for wide-lined
   notebooks,

And for the computers that enable us to keep in touch
   with the people we care about,

Wherever they may be.

And let us thank God for the iPods and the iPads

And all the other gadgets that we do not yet know how
   to use,

But that we hope to master one of these days.

Let us thank God for the atheists and the agnostics,

Who keep us from believing without thinking,

And who make us prove our faith by the way we live.

And let us thank God for thankfulness,

Which enriches our lives so much,

Whenever we remember to feel it.

Thank You, God, for being You,

And thank You, God, for enabling us to be ourselves.

Fill Our Days with Hints of Paradise

Danny Siegel

Lord—

Fill our days with hints of paradise.

Let us see Adam and Eve
in everyone we meet.

Let Wednesdays point to eternity
and cloudy mornings remind us of Sinai.

You are gracious unto us:

How much do we pay
for the evening sunsets?
What is the price of the stars?

Our Silences of Love

Danny Siegel

O God, You are a consolation to Your creatures,
For in moments of forgetting,
We but call to mind Your care, and we are comforted.
When we hope no more,
A pattern in the sand reminds us of Your love.
Your dawns give us confidence, and sleep is a friend.
Our sorrows dissipate in the presence of an infant's smile,
And old men's words revive our will-to-wish.
Your hints are everywhere,
Your signals in the most remote of places.
You are here;
We fail words to say, "*Mah tov!*"
How good our breath,
Our rushing energies,
Our silences of love.

What I Am Not Thankful For

Rabbi David Wolpe

I am not thankful for stings and slights we each bear,
not thankful for the small pettiness embroidered in our
   characters.
I am not grateful, Dear God, for the hurts that plague us.
I cannot thank You for the ways, large and small, that
   we scar our neighbor's hearts,
Coax tears from angry eyes
Wound those whom we love,
Shame and hurt one another.
But my God, my rock, I am grateful that You help us to
   see;
So we can heal, soothe sorrows, ease pain,
Raise those who are bowed down.
We are thankful for blessings, O Lord, but also for the
   gift of giving blessing.

For Sustaining Us

Thank You for Lowering My Voice

Rabbi Ben Kamin

Sweet God, thank You for providing me with the
    therapy of failure
So that I might learn from You the meaning of success.
Thank You for burnishing contrition into my daily
    thoughts
And for making me increasingly unimpressed with myself.
Thank You for degrading the value of a byline
In favor of a not just walking by
Another person
Who looked to me for substance and not schmaltz.
Thank You for providing me with a second chance
To live a life of purposeful creativity
Rather than for the purpose of creating an image.
Thank You for lowering my voice
And for guiding me to the wisdom of silence.
Thank You for helping me to turn the page
And to actually read the transcripts of other people's
    pain
But even more so for instructing me to realize
That You created us one by one

And not for making me the one.

Thank You for being patient with my need for
attention

And for nudging me to the attention of others

And their cogent words and healing hands and quiet
accomplishments

That surpass all the noise I used to make;

That I pray You now receive as a glad sound.

God of Lonely Hours

Yehuda Karni, translated by Rabbi Chaim Stern

God of lonely hours,
God holy and awesome,
   who breathed my puzzled Jewish soul
     (so apparent, and so hidden)
   within me,
     and kindled within me the human light
   in all its colors;
God who made me an emblem
   for my age;
at dusk, dawn, noon
You grind me with desert stone, sand and with
sweet promise of grapes that will be wine,
   You lure me, and
hang me over the abyss of my own depths
   day after day—
Don't now disappear,
You who keep me whole:
Be with me.
Gather my blossoms falling at Your feet,
my honest thanks
   for Your love
   and being's wonder.

A Prayer for Rosh Hashanah

Danny Maseng

I wish not to beg You for anything anymore. I wish to thank You. I wish to be a grateful lover, not a chastised child. This pleading with You makes me infantile. It is unbecoming.

I wish not to place you on a pedestal as I would an idol. I wish to speak to You face to face, to dwell in Your house, to taste the earth that is filled with Your glory in this very human mouth of mine.

I wish to go into the days of awe in wonder, awestricken—not trembling and fearing for my life or for the lives of those I love. I wish to be in perpetual awe of the beauty of Your world. The very world I live in, with its horror and heartbreaks, with its disappointments and misgivings, with its splendor and grandeur, with its nakedness and its garments, with its truth and consequences—this very world I see before me right now, at this very moment.

I wish to leave the future world and its constructions to futurists, alchemists, and theorists. I'll settle for the one I'm in right now, the one that You are in right now, the world that keeps coming over and over again with no thought of future or past. I like this awful, awesome world. I am very grateful for it.

I wish to thank You for every moment lived until this very breath I take at this very moment of breathless gratitude. I shall be forever grateful at this very moment for all of Your deeds and thoughts, most of which are beyond my comprehension, which was never that great to begin with and is fading, thank God, day by day.

This is the day God made—let us rejoice in it! This is the moment of creation, the moment all becomes possible, when all that can ever be is present, is a present, and I wish only to be present at such an awesome moment.

A Prayer

Rabbi Ralph D. Mecklenburger

Dear God,
though we never run out of things to complain about,
we do know that we are richly blessed in countless ways.
There are family and friends, the fine food we enjoy
and too often take for granted,
our warm homes, political freedoms,
and so much more.
For meaningful work, the beauties of Your world,
the people whose labor, and often whose love and
compassion,
sustain and benefit us daily, we thank You.
For all the things for which, even now, we forget to be
grateful,
for life itself and every blessings which gives it quality,
we praise You. Amen.

A Prayer

Rabbi Ralph D. Mecklenburger

For islands of sanity, O God, in a world awash in hostility, we are grateful. Help us, we pray, through learning and continued joint effort, to build bridges of understanding. Fill us with idealism and the courage of our convictions. Inspire us to exemplify appreciation for diversity and love of all Your children. Amen.

A Prayer of Gratitude

Rabbi Warren Stone

Source of all blessings
I am Grateful
for my life
for the Blessings
of
my breath
the beating of my heart
Source of all blessings
I am Grateful
for Beloved Ones who
share life with me
those in our world beside me
and those in worlds beyond my knowing
Source of all blessings
I am grateful
to share life with our human family
Jewish, Christian, Moslem, Buddhist, Hindu, Sikh
May we walk gently upon our Earth
Source of all blessings
I am grateful
to be one with all creation
the flight of birdwings
the swirling of blueshoals oceans deep

the runnings of wilderness creatures
the sway of forests green
Source of all blessing
I am grateful
to be part of the spiraling
of all space and time
beyond my imagination
Yes and again Yes I am grateful
to always be here
where else could I go?
For all this and more
I am grateful

Tzur Mishelo Achalnu

Translated by Rabbi Zalman Schachter-Shalomi

HaShem, You fed us dinner
Let us all give thanks
We ate and are sated
The gift of Your hands

You nurture us and others
Our Shepherd and our Host
We ate of Your bounty
And drank of Your vineyards
Now we give our thank-Yous
With the mouth that ate Your food
Singing and praising
Your holy repute

We sing to You our God
We offer You our thanks
For earth and her harvest
With which we are gifted
Our souls are also glad
For the plenty that we had
Your love fills our being
Your truth fills our mind

We need Your kind attention
So needy are Your folk

To come to Your Temple
On Zion's holy Hill
May David's heir redeem us
May he soon arrive
We long for his redeeming
To reinvigorate our life.

Your holy house rebuild now
Let Zion's streets be filled
New music will we make
New songs we all will sing
Compassionate of Blessings
We sing to You our grace
And raise our cup of thankfulness
For Your presence in our lives.

Asher Eimatcha (Though Your Dread)
Translated by Rabbi Mishael Zion

Though Your dread is upon
The faithful angels
Who are intensely loyal
Who are courageous knights
And Your dread is upon them.

Yet You desire praise
From clods of earth
From those of putrid deeds
Who are sated with rage
Who are devoid of truth
Who are empty of justice
And this is Your praise!
You desire praise
From weak mortals
From mere breath and chaos
From wilted flowers
From passing shadows—
And therein lies Your praise!

Redemption

A Prayer for the Returned Traveler

Rabbi Daniel F. Polish

Dear God whose name is written on the doorposts of my house

Now that the road of my journeys has led me back to where I started, I thank You for all that I encountered on my travels: all the sights I have seen, all the things I have done, and all the things I have learned. Thank You for the joy of discovery and the excitement of the journey. Thank You for the ways I have grown from my travels. And thank You, above all, for the privilege of being returned safely to my own home, and lying again in my own bed.

Prayer for When You Are Recuperating from an Illness, Under the Weather, or Just Giving Yourself Some Time Off
(Or Prayer for When You Take Refuge in Your Bed)

Rabbi Daniel F. Polish

I am not by my lathe
I am not in my field
I am not at my desk
I am—
   Surrounded by the most familiar things in my life—
In my bed
   The most comforting place that I know
And I am grateful for that
Rofei kol basar, I thank You.

Thanksgiving Day

Thanksgiving Day

Rabbi Sidney Greenberg

We thank You, O God, for our family and for what we mean and bring to one another. We are grateful for the bonds of loyalty and affection that sustain us and keep us close to one another no matter how far apart we may be. We thank You for implanting within us a deep need for each other and giving us the capacity to love and to care. Help us to be modest in our demands of one another, but generous in our giving to each other. May we never measure how much love or encouragement we offer; may we never count the times we forgive. Rather, may we always be grateful that we have one another and that we are able to express our love in acts of kindness. Keep us gentle in our speech. When we offer words of criticism, may they be chosen with care and spoken softly. May we waste no opportunity to speak words of sympathy, of appreciation, of praise. Bless our family with health, happiness, and contentment. Above all, grant us the wisdom to build a joyous and peaceful home in which Your spirit will always abide. Amen.

Waking Up

Modeh Ani L'fanecha

Rabbi James B. Rosenberg

Modeh ani l'fanecha, I give thanks to You
Who wakes me into soft morning light
Who spreads out the tent of the sky
Who flames the day with sunflower faces

Who wakes me into soft morning light
As gulls scream their hunger in loud, soaring flight
Who flames the day with sunflower faces
Burning and yearning for the death of the night

As gulls scream their hunger in loud, soaring flight
Who spreads out the tent of the sky
Burning and yearning for the death of the night
Modeh ani l'fanecha, I give thanks to You.

Immortality

Rabbi Robert Scheinberg

Each morning You restore consciousness to my sleep-filled body, and I awake.

Each spring You restore vitality to trees, plants, and animals that have hibernated through the winter, and they grow once more.

Each moment I contemplate the rebirth of our people; I recall that You put the breath of life into dry bones.

Praised are You, Adonai, for planting immortality in my soul, in my people, and in our world.

Nature

Blessings of Pleasure
Rabbi Adam D. Fisher

I.

Seeing
green waves roll
peak
pound down
pull back
suck into themselves
rise up again
   I praise You
   who made the great sea.

Skin soft white dogwood petals
white cherry clusters
pink nectarine blossoms
magenta wygelia
yellow forsythia sprays
   I praise You
   who placed such beauty
   in Your world.

II.
Hearing
rolling cracking
thunder,
wind screaming
thunder,
waterfalls pounding
thunder,
    I praise You
    whose awesome might rumbles
    through the world.

III.
Smelling
scrub oak and birch woods
spongy mulch
pungent after a rain,
pitch pines on sandy barrens
tang of juniper berries
    I praise You
    for creating fragrant woods.

Heavy scented lilacs
cut roses in a vase,
lemon balm lavender
summer marigolds
my hands after picking tomatoes,
    I praise You
      for creating fragrant plants.

Ripe cantaloupe
watermelon cut,
apricots dried
apples baking,
cider just pressed
bushels of farmstand peaches,
    I praise You
      who gives fragrance to fruit.

Ginger tarragon cinnamon fennel
Sweet basil marjoram cumin cloves
    I praise You
      for piquant spices.

Peanut sesame olive oils in the kitchen
perfumes of musk,
coconut oil smoothed on bodies at the beach
neat's-foot for a baseball glove,
    I praise You
      for aromatic oils.

IV.
Tasting
a crust of rye or wheat
inside textured with seeds
a pinch of salt,
    I praise You
    who brings forth bread.

Soft smooth cream colored banana
red raspberries full of seeds
a section of a navel orange
    juice on my chin
cold grapes
    plucked from the stem,
    I praise You
    who creates luscious fruit.

God of Creation

Rabbi Roy A. Walter

Lord, God of color!
God of yellow dawns and orange dusks,
Of plush green fields and cracked brown river beds,
Of blue skies and gray clouds.
God of rich, black earth and the white snow that
    covers it,
Of golden sunshine and clear, lucid raindrops.

Lord, God of shapes!
God of pentagons and hexagons and squares,
Of elliptical orbits and triangular cones,
Of perfect circles and imperfect squares.
God of trapezoids and rectangles and straight lines and
    curves.

Lord, God of sizes!
God of giant sequoias and tiny bacteria,
Of bottomless caverns and lofty mountain peaks,
Of mustard seeds and acorns and spores.
God of heights and depth and breadth.

Lord, God of creation!
God of everything that inhabits the earth,
And the earth itself!
Thank You for all Your creation with its endless variety,
And for our senses with which we perceive the myriad of
    Your creation.

A Blessing for the Twilight

Rabbi Reuben Zellman

As the sun sinks and the colors of the day turn, we offer a blessing for the twilight, for twilight is neither day nor night, but in between. We are all twilight people. We can never be fully labeled or defined. We are many identities and loves, many genders and none. We are in between roles at, the intersection of histories, or between place and place. We are crisscrossed paths of memory and destination, streaks of light swirled together. We are neither day nor night. We are both, neither, and all.

May the sacred in-between of this evening suspend our certainties, soften our judgment, and widen our vision. May this in-between light illuminate our way to the God who transcends all categories and definitions. May the in-between people who have come to pray be lifted up into this twilight. We cannot always define; we can always say a blessing. Blessed are You, God of all, who brings on the twilight.

Legacy

Planning for the Future

You and I Plant Trees

Rabbi Bradley Shavit Artson (abridged)

You and I plant trees, Ancient One,

And then nourish them where they sprout—

Reaching toward the light,

Burrowing to the Source,

Eternally entwined, complete.

A Prayer upon Finding Oneself in Miami Beach and Saying, "Hey, We Should Retire Here …"

Rabbi Jeffrey Salkin

Blessed are You, Source of the generations,

God of Abraham, God of Isaac, God of Jacob

God of Sarah, God of Rebecca, God of Rachel and Leah,

God of George and Sid, Max and Harriet, Joseph and Rose,

God of the ones whose names I have forgotten

God of the ones who sit mutely in sepia photographs

God who puts words in my mouth that echo those of the generations that came before me

O God, who awakens me in the morning and places me before the mirror

And who forces me to see my father's face

Blessed are You, Adonai, who teaches me, day by day,

That what happens to the parents happens to the children.

Slowly, and in its own way.

Peace

Beyond

Dan Nichols (adapted)

May Your wonder be celebrated, may Your name be
consecrated.

May Your brilliance never fade, from the magnificent
world You made.

May Your ways prevail in our own days, in our own
lives.

And in the life of all Israel.

May Your name receive the same beauty that You
bring.

Though You are far beyond the sweetest song we could
ever sing.

And let us say: Amen.

A Prayer for Peace

Rabbi Nachman of Breslov

Lord of peace, Divine Ruler, to whom peace belongs.
Master of peace, Creator of all things.

May it be Thy will to put an end to war and bloodshed
on earth, and to spread a great and wonderful peace
over the whole world, so that nation shall not lift
up sword against nation, neither shall they learn war
anymore.

Help us and save us all, and let us cling tightly to the
virtue of peace. Let there be a truly great peace
between every person and their fellow, and between
husband and wife, and let there be no discord
between people even in their hearts.

Let us never shame any person on earth, great or
small. May it be granted unto us to fulfill Thy
commandment to "Love thy neighbor as thyself,"
with all our hearts and souls and bodies and
possessions.

And let it come to pass in our time as it is written,
"And I will give peace in the land, and you shall lie
down and none shall make you afraid. I will drive
the wild beasts from the land, and neither shall the
sword go through your land."

God who is peace, bless us with peace.

Peace Prayer

Rabbi Rami M. Shapiro

We call upon the Source and Substance of all reality,
to open our bodies, hearts, and minds to the divine
manifest in and as all beings.

We pray for peace: peace in our hearts, peace in our
homes, peace in our communities, for only in this
way can we make peace in the world.

We pray for the safety of combatants and
noncombatants alike. May they see in each other
not friend or foe, but fellow humans sharing a
commonality truer and deeper than the surface
differences we mistake for ontological divisions.

We pray for spaciousness of mind
to know that diversity is divinity manifest in time and
space.

We pray for spaciousness of heart
to know that love is greater than fear.

We pray for the humility
to know we do not know.

We pray for the courage to question our certainties.

We pray for the strength to put down our prejudices.

We pray for the clarity to see in the other the infinitely
faceted Face of God.

We pray for the grace to awaken to the truth of One
God, One Humanity, One World, and One Moral
Code: justice and compassion for all.

May each of us attend to the deepest and best within us
that we might weave the diverse and unique threads of
our lives
into a universal tapestry of wisdom, kindness, and
peace.

We ask for this in all Your names: those we know and
those we do not;
those we can speak and those we cannot; those we
remember and those we have forgotten; those we
are taught and those we have yet to learn; and in
that Great Name beyond naming: the silence that
embraces all things in wonder.

Nature

A Post-Hurricane Prayer

Rabbi Samuel Barth

Esa enai el heharim—me'ayin yavo ezri? "I lift my eyes to the high places—where will my help come from?"

Your power, God, Creator of the world, is manifest in the winds of the hurricane and the destruction they cause. We turn to You to pray for the wisdom and strength of those responsible for preparation and rescue, for administration and coordination, the first and last responders. May they find the strength and courage, the insight and judgment, the love of humanity to do their best to bring our wisdom and technology to alleviate suffering, to heal injury, and to restore the services and infrastructure upon which our lives are built. And may we all find ourselves ready to give support, encouragement, love, and gifts as needed.

Ezri me'im Adonai, oseh shamayim va'aretz; "My help comes from Adonai who made the heavens and the earth."

Prayer in the Wake of the Tsunami

Rabbi Shai Held

Ruler of Creation, Master of the world:

Have mercy on all those who are suffering from the raging waters and the storming waves.

Have compassion on Your creatures—Look, O Lord, and see their distress;

Listen, God, and hear their cries.

Strengthen the hands of those who would bring relief, comfort the mourners,

Heal, please, the wounded.

Grant us wisdom and discernment to know our obligations,

and open our hearts so that we may extend our hands to the devastated.

Bless us so that we may walk in Your ways,

"compassionate ones, children of compassionate ones."

Grant us the will and the wisdom to prevent further disaster and death;

Prevent plague from descending upon Your earth, and fulfill Your words,

"Never again shall there be another flood to destroy the earth."

Amen. So may it be Your will.

A Post-Storm Prayer

Rabbi David A. Ingber

Source of all life, soothe hearts aching with pain and
loss.

Source of compassion, support all of those who
are confused and bewildered in the wake of this
shocking storm.

Mysterious One, move within all of our hearts to help
and support one another as we comfort and care for
those who are in need. Master of all healing, heal all
who desperately need a *refuah shleimah*, a full healing
in body, heart, mind, and spirit.

Ana El na, refa na lanu; please, loving Source, please
heal us.

Amen.

Prayer for Flood-Filled Days

Rabbi Paul J. Kipnes

Eloheinu v'Elohei avoteinu v'imoteinu,
Our God and God of our fathers and mothers,
The flood waters came, wreaking havoc upon our cities,
  our homes,
our rescue workers, our sense of security,
And we turn to You for comfort and support.
Help us to differentiate between floods of destruction
and down-pouring of Your love and comfort.

We know that waters can destroy.
In a world decimated many times before,
having been submerged in waters from the Florida
  hurricanes, the Asian tsunami, and ...
each of biblical proportions,
we remember the destructive abilities of these flood
  waters.

Recalling now that the world, though filled with Your
  Glory,
is not equal to Your flawlessness,
we strive desperately, sometimes without success,
to move beyond the impulse to blame You.

Keep us far from apocalyptic thoughts, for we know
that You ask us to care for each other, an awesome
responsibility.

We also know that we can seek You in the waters.
We recall Your Loving Hand, guiding us in our infancy:

From a barren rock, You brought forth water to quench
our thirst,
In the midst of a journey through the wilderness, You
showed Miriam a
myriad of wells which healed our parched throats,
You guided us through *Yam Suf*, the Red Sea, moving
us past destruction
toward new life and new beginnings.
Through Your love, we found our way.

Be with us now, during these deluged days.

Draw us close to those harmed by these waters, hearing
their
cries, responding to their needs.
Lead us to support those who will fix the cities,
care for the displaced, who bring healing to those
suffering.

Though our attention spans seem so short, may we
be slow to forget those who were in danger.

Please bring a warm wind and hot sun from the
    heavenly realms
to help dry up the flood waters.

And may we all embrace at least one lesson spoken
    aloud by so many who—facing the floods—rushed to
    pack up their valuables:

That memories of love and of time spent with family
    and friends
    are priceless, holy and sacred.
This can never be taken away.
As we rush to meet the challenge of living in this
    imperfect world of ours,
May we slow down enough to cherish those who are
    truly valuable—
kadosh/holy—to us.

Baruch atah Adonai, hamavdil bein kodesh l'chol.
Blessed are You, O God, who differentiates between
    the truly valuable and everything else.

Prayer for Those in Harm's Way of a Storm

Rabbi Andy Koren (adapted)

Avinu shebashamayim—God of the heavens: nature and all that You have created are truly awesome. Often, we take these wonders for granted. Teach us to cherish all of Your gifts.

Try as we might, we know that we cannot control the oceans, the mountains, the weather. We also firmly believe that ever since the time of Noah, You do not send floods, make the earth shake, or dispatch weather formations, such as hurricanes, as warnings or punishments.

So we ask, as this storm is approaching land—and approaching our brothers and sisters there—that You shelter all who will be in its path. Watch over everyone—loved ones, friends, and fellow people, many of whom are preparing to evacuate. Guard them as they prepare, perhaps to leave their homes—again. Give them strength, courage, and resolve to ride out this storm; answer their prayers and ours that they be blessed with goodness and be spared from harm.

Blessed are You, Source of life and nature, whose awesome power and strength fill our world and inspire us to be strong in the face of all of life's difficulties. Amen.

Grace

Rabbi Abraham Danziger (adapted)

Master of the Universe

Is there a person anywhere who never sins?

I am but flesh and blood, often yielding to temptation

I am human, often torn by conflicts.

You created me with ears

So I could listen to Your world and Your word,

But instead I have listened to gossip and words of
   hatred …

You created me with a tongue and a mouth

And gave them the ability to speak …

But [I just] embarrassed people, laughed at others,
   gossiped, lied, and

caused arguments.

You created me with hands, with the ability to transmit
   tenderness and

comfort

But I have often used my hands for hurting others.

You created me with legs to walk in the path of
   holiness,

But I have used them to run to do frivolous things.

… [Therefore, I] devote this day to asking forgiveness
   for the misuse of

Your gifts during this past year, and to learn once again
   the holiness of my

body.

Psalm 93
An Interpretive Translation

Rabbi Edward Feld

Entwined in worlds,
enwrapped in glory,
    You are.
So it has been,
and so it is—
    eternally You are.
Waves pounding out their
song reach up to God
from their depths,
    for the song of the sea,
    beaten to the sound of
    the breakers, tells of the
    God within.
These are proof enough
for the faithful—that You
are the lord of time.

Prayer following *Kol Nidre* Service

Rabbi Arthur Green

Lord of the World,
I stand before You
And before my fellow humans
Pardoning, forgiving
All those who have hurt or angered me
Or sinned against me.

Whether this hurt was one of
Bodily harm,
Financial loss,
A wound to my honor,
Or anything else that's mine—

Whether the other was forced to hurt me
Or did so willingly,
Whether by accident or intent,
Whether I was harmed by word or by deed,
Whether this wound is a new one
Or one left over from some earlier world of mine—

I forgive because we are both human.

May no person be held guilty on my account.

Hear My Prayer

Harold Kohn

Eternal Spirit,
God of the heavens above
And of the earth below,
God of drifting clouds
And of leaping, laughing streams,
Hear my prayer.

As every river is conceived by clouds,
And every stream begins in rain,
So may my every thought come from above
And my every purpose have its origin in You.

We Can't Ask You

Rabbi Harold S. Kushner

We can't pray that You make our lives free of problems; this won't happen and it is probably just as well. We can't ask You to make us and those we love immune to disease, because You can't do that. We can't ask You to weave a magic spell around us so that bad things will only happen to other people, and never to us…. But people who pray for courage, for strength to bear the unbearable, for the grace to remember what they have left instead of what they have lost, very often find their prayers answered. They discover that they have more strength, more courage than they ever knew themselves to have.

Let the Rain Come

Rabbi Harold S. Kushner

Let the rain come and wash away the ancient grudges,
the bitter hatreds, held and nourished over
generations.

Let the rain wash away the memory of the hurt, and
the neglect.

Then let the sun come and fill the sky with rainbows.

Let the warmth of the sun heal us wherever we are
broken.

Let it burn away the fog, so that we can see each other
clearly,

So that we can see beyond labels, beyond accents,
gender, or skin color.

Let the warmth and the brightness of the sun melt our
selfishness, so that we can share the joys and sorrows
of our neighbors.

And let the light of the sun be so strong that we will
see all people as neighbors.

Let the earth, nourished by rain, bring forth flowers to
surround us with beauty.

And let the mountains teach our hearts to reach
upward to heaven. Amen.

Set Me as a Seal

Danny Maseng

Set me as a seal upon your heart
A seal upon your arm
Upon your eyes
A stumbling block before the blind
Set a fire in your heart
A flame upon your hands
A torch beneath your feet
Ignite me in your dreams
Consume me in your thirst
Make firewater dance
Walk gently on the coals
Resuscitate your secret name
Repeat to me in tongues again
Demand again
Remove me into wild meadows
Brand me with your eyes like wayward sheep
Leave deep and everlasting marks between my gates
Like frontlets on my doorposts
Falcons on my shoulders
Like turtle doves
Make sure the mark is seen
Make sure the wax is hot
Be sure the deed is done

Let no one be uncertain
Cast me by the roadside
Like a fallen marker
Like a tattered map
Like a tethered dream
A broken wing
A fallen moon
Like an empty river
Like a seal upon your heart
Like a seal upon your outstretched arm

On Being with Constricted Jewish People and Concepts

Jay Michaelson

God of loving-kindness,
I have come across a word, a person, a thought,
among the holy tongue and people Israel,
which brings me uncertainty and pain.
All the familiar tensions arise:
separation, fear of separation,
contradiction, judgment of myself and others,
questioning, again, the path of my ancestors,
and the fruits it brings today.

Merciful One,
help me to see clearly.
Help me to judge others and myself less.
Help me return to Your presence,
in this present moment,
from which springs the love we seek.
From this place of communion,
recall in me the goodness within us,
and that even the most twisted-up shape of mind
still carries within it the impulse to be happy.

For the concepts I cannot accept,
grant me the peace of setting aside without anger.

For the people by whom I feel attacked,
grant me the delight of surrender.
I do not own You, holy one.
I do not own Judaism.
I do not own the right opinion.

God, grant me the freedom from the desire to convince.

Let the constrictions loosen and drop away
Let all beings be happy
Let us relax these fixations with form
… starting with me.

Why Am I So Hated by My Enemies?

Rabbi James L. Mirel

Why am I so hated and despised by my enemies?

What have I done to be so attacked and persecuted?

God be with me and help me remember that when I ask
questions like these I fall into the trap that my
enemies have set for me.

I have done nothing to deserve enmity. While I
acknowledge my shortcomings and mistakes, I know
that I am worthy of love and respect.

Let me not internalize my enemies' irrational and
destructive feelings for me.

Let me remember that it is *their* need to hate that
motivates them.

They may hurt me, they may slay me—but only if I let
their view of me become my own can they defeat me.

If my enemies make me become self-hating, bitter,
angry, or cynical—then they have won.

Let me rise above their anger and help me to keep in
mind Your Eternal Love for me which will sustain me
even if I am disdained and ridiculed.

Help me to affirm: I am a child of God and worthy of
Love—Divine and human.

Reb Noson's *Likutey Tefilot* Prayer 44

Translated by Yaakov David Shulman

HaShem my God, God of Abraham, Isaac and Jacob, help me always to pray to You with all my heart and spirit; with powerful intent; with true holiness; with purity and faith; with awe, love and clarity. Free my mind of foreign thoughts. May all my prayers take place on holy ground. May I sanctify the ground on which I stand so that it is as holy as the Land of Israel. Awaken my heart to pray to You with awesome inspiration, until my hands are so invigorated that I raise them up to You and clap them together in joy and wondrous animation for the sake of Your Name alone.

A Prayer upon Knowing That I, Too, Am Israel

Rabbi Jeffrey Salkin

> *Baruch atah Adonai, Eloheinu Melech ha'olam, she'asani Yisrael.*
>
> Blessed is Adonai, who has made me Yisrael.
>
> Blessed is Adonai, who made me Yisrael by first making me Jacob:
>
> Blessed the Jacob within me, who is capable of deception,
>
> Blessed the Jacob within me, who dreams of a ladder to heaven,
>
> Blessed is the Yisrael within me, who wrestles inwardly and outwardly,
>
> Blessed is the Yisrael within me, who seeks wholeness and redemption.
>
> Blessed is *am Yisrael* within me,
> The piece of me that knows the whole story:
> Enslavement, freedom, revelation of truth,
> betrayal of ideals, wandering in a wilderness,
> complaining, and homecoming.

Prayer for Yom Kippur *Katan*
Rabbi Zalman Schachter-Shalomi

You my God, my Helper
Ordering my life is not easy
My struggles before You.

Keep at my side as I strive
I am not as good as I wish to be
Put forth Your light and lead me
Please guide my steps on Your path
Up to the level I can live on
Raise my actions to my values.

Kindness plant in my heart
Attention to the ways I am relating
To others who cross my path
And help me live in balance
Neither in haste nor in sloth.

And give me joy in Your service
Making bright the lives
Of my loved ones
Embracing the lot You give me
Morning, noon, and night
In Your service.

How may I come to You
If I did not heed Your word?

What You have made pure
I have polluted.
What You have loved
I despised.

What You have ordered
I have disrupted.
What You have intended
I have opposed.
Take my ways and turn them
So that I might make pure.

What I have polluted
That I may love what You love
That I may set to order what I have disrupted
That I might intend what You intend
May I be renewed
Like the moon.

May I reflect Your light
Ever waxing.

Borrowed
A Prayer to Live with Grace

Rabbi Rami M. Shapiro

May we discover through pain and torment
the strength to live with grace and humor.
May we discover through doubt and anguish
the strength to live with dignity and holiness.
May we discover through suffering and fear
the strength to move toward healing.
May it come to pass that we be restored to health and
   to vigor.
May life grant us wellness of body, spirit, and mind.
And if this cannot be so, may we find in this
   transformation and passage
moments of meaning, opportunities for love and the
   deep and gracious calm
that comes when we allow ourselves to move on.

A Prayer following the *Amidah*

Rabbi Elazar, translated by Danny Siegel

May it be Your will, O God, our God,
to grace our lives with love and friendship and peace,
and a feeling of the intimacy with all humanity
and may the borders of our lives overflow with
    students,
and may our end be exceptionally hopeful
and may our ultimate place be in paradise,
and arrange things so that, in this, Your world,
we will have good friends and have the disposition to
    do good,
and allow us to awaken with our yearnings fulfilled to
    be in awe of Your name,
and may our happiness be pleasing in Your presence.

All Is God

YOU!

Rabbi James B. Rosenberg

> … and a man wrestled with him
> until the break of dawn.
>
> GENESIS 32:25

You elude me like a name heard once.
You taunt me with demands I cannot meet
And cannot fail to meet.
Shall I strip off my anger like a bathing suit
   coarse with sand?
Shall I swallow my lust like a vitamin?
You call me to a yesterday I cannot face
And to a tomorrow far deeper than the river
   I have crossed.
Your sweaty arms drip insolence.
Your bony legs squeeze me to truth.

You! You! You!

Psalm 95

Rabbi Rami M. Shapiro

It is all You:
the valleys, the mountains
and shore and the sea,
it is all You.
And so am I—
This fragile reed
with beating heart and jumping mind;
this thinking bellows
breathed and breathing,
all You.
From You comes each
and to You each returns.
And in between is You as well.
You in anger and You in song,
You in play and You in pain,
You in danger and You in salvation;
it is all You and You are all it is.
I sing the wonders of all You are
and the simple truth of You is known.

Acknowledgments

We met about twenty-five years ago under the auspices of the Morris Zimmerman Memorial Institute, sponsored by Hebrew Union College–Jewish Institute of Religion. This institute—which was copied by many institutions in the years that followed—was a pioneer effort in that it affirmed the value of profound prayer and in-depth study in a liberal Jewish religious context. From that beginning grew years of working together and learning together. This collection of men's prayers is among the many fruits of those efforts.

But this is not just the work of two men. At best, we are merely the channels of those who seek a more profound relationship with the Divine.

We want to thank those who humbly made suggestions of the works of others to be included in this book. We also want to thank those whose personal prayers—profound outpourings of the heart—were not included because they didn't fit the parameters established for this volume. It certainly does not diminish our appreciation for their words or their recommendations. In particular, we thank Rabbi Steve

Booth-Nadav, Rabbi Edward Boraz, Marty Cohen, Rabbi Susan Einbinder, Rabbi Robert Eisen, Dr. Eitan Fishbane, Jeff Friedman, Moshe Giventhal, Mitch Gordon, Robert Grayson, Rabbi Baruch HaLevi, Rabbi Bradley Hirschfield, Rabbi Elie Kaufner, Rabbi Allan Lehmann, Rabbi David Lyon, Rabbi Eliot Malomet, Rabbi Bernard Mehlman, Rabbi Harvey Meirovich, Dr. Jerred Metz, Rabbi Michelle Missaghieh, Lev Natan, Rabbi Danny Nevins, Rabbi Dennis Ross, Justin Sakofs, Rabbi Neil Sandler, Howard Schwartz, Rabbi Charles Simon, Rabbi Gordon Tucker, Rabbi Abraham Twerski, Rabbi Michael Unger, and Robert Unger. We also want to thank Jeremy Katz, Kevin Profitt, and Rabbi Gary Zola at the American Jewish Archives for recommending some classic prayers among historical American Jewish leaders. We had many wonderful and insightful conversations about this book with so many people; we apologize if we neglected to publicly thank all of them by name. Please forgive us.

We also want to thank the people at Jewish Lights Publishing who truly understand that the creation of a book is a work of art. It is also a prayer unto itself. In particular, we thank the partnership of Emily Wichland, who edited the volume, and Kaitlin Johnstone, who assisted with the editing and review process. Adapting the words of the Rabbis of the Talmud, we offer these words: May the words of our mouths and the meditations of our hearts be acceptable unto You, our Rock and Redeemer.

KMO and SMM

About the Contributors

Israel Abrahams (1858–1925) was a British scholar who taught homiletics at Jews College in London and Talmud at Cambridge University.

Aharon of Karlin (1802–1872) was a famous Hasidic rabbi in northwestern Russia.

Daniel S. Alexander is rabbi of Congregation Beth Israel in Charlottesville, Virginia.

Alexandri (third century CE) was one of two Talmudic Rabbis from the Land of Israel of the same name.

Bezalel Aloni is managing director and producer of Piano Music in Israel.

Bradley Shavit Artson, DHL, rabbi, is the Abner and Roslyn Goldstine Dean's Chair of the Ziegler School of Rabbinic Studies at American Jewish University in Los Angeles, California.

Samuel Barth, rabbi, is senior lecturer in liturgy at The Jewish Theological Seminary of America.

Hillel Bavli (1893–1961) was a Hebrew poet, author, and professor of Hebrew literature at The Jewish Theological Seminary of America.

Shye Ben-Tzur is an Israeli *qawwali* singer who composes *qawwalis* (Sufi devotional music popular in South Asia) in Hebrew.

Chaim Nachman Bialik (1873–1934) was a Russian-born Hebrew poet and essayist.

Sheldon H. Blank (1896–1989), PhD, rabbi, was a professor of Bible at Hebrew Union College–Jewish Institute of Religion, Cincinnati, Ohio.

Ben Zion Bokser (1907–1984) was a major figure in the Conservative rabbinate and an advocate of social justice.

Harold Braunstein lives in Brighton Beach, Brooklyn, New York.

Daniel S. Brenner is a Reconstructionist rabbi who is director of initiatives for boys at Moving Traditions in Philadelphia, Pennsylvania.

Eliezer Bugatin is a Hebrew poet.

Shlomo Carlebach (1925–1994) was a rabbi, musician, and founder of the House of Love and Peace in San Francisco, California.

Avraham Chalfi (1904–1980) was an Israeli actor and poet.

Mike Comins, rabbi, is founder of Torah Trek: The Center for Jewish Wilderness Spirituality.

Howard Cooper, rabbi, is director of spiritual development at Finchley Reform Synagogue in Great Britain.

Menachem Creditor, rabbi, is the spiritual leader of Congregation Netivot Shalom in Berkeley, CA; author of the poetry collection *Fissures and Love*; and editor of *Peace in Our Cities: Rabbi Against Gun Violence*. His latest musical recording is "Within." He blogs at www.menachemcreditor.org

Abraham Danziger (1748–1820), rabbi, was a contemporary of Rabbi Nachman and author of *Chayei Adam*.

Harry K. Danziger is rabbi emeritus of Temple Israel in Memphis, Tennessee.

Elazar (end of first century CE), although mentioned by his first name, was probably Elazar ben Azariah, teacher in the Talmud, whose name is also mentioned in the Haggadah for Pesach.

Elimelech of Lizhensk (1717–1787) was one of the great founding rabbis of the Hasidic movement, in Poland.

Dov Peretz Elkins, formerly rabbi at the Princeton Jewish Center in New Jersey, is founder of Growth Associates.

Abraham ibn Ezra (1089–1164) was a Spanish rabbi who is recognized as one of the most distinguished philosophers of the Middle Ages.

Morley T. Feinstein is rabbi of the University Synagogue in Los Angeles, California.

Edward Feld is a rabbi who served as editor of *Mahzor Lev Shalem*, the High Holy Day prayer book for the Conservative movement.

Mordecai Finley is rabbi of Ohr Hatorah in Los Angeles, California.

Adam D. Fisher is rabbi emeritus at Temple Isaiah in Stony Brook, New York.

Ira Flax is rabbi for youth and education at Temple Beth El in Birmingham, Alabama.

Solomon ibn Gabirol (1021–1058) was a Spanish-Jewish philosopher and Hebrew poet.

Elihu Gevirtz has worked as a professional biologist and land-use planner in Southern and Central California and subsequently studied for the rabbinate at the Academy for Jewish Religion in Los Angeles, California.

Jeffrey Goldwasser is rabbi of Temple Beit HaYam in Stuart, Florida.

James Stone Goodman, musician and poet, is rabbi of Congregation Neve Shalom in Creve Coeur, Missouri.

Arthur Green, rabbi, is Irving Brudnick Professor of Jewish Philosophy and rector of the Rabbinical School at Hebrew College in Newton, Massachusetts.

Sidney Greenberg (1917–2003) was rabbi of Temple Sinai in Dresher, Pennsylvania, for over fifty years.

Judah HaLevi (1075–1141) was a Spanish liturgical poet and author of *The Kuzari*.

Jules Harlow, rabbi and liturgist, edited the prayer books for the Conservative movement, including the *Sim Shalom* series.

Shai Held, rabbi, is cofounder, *rosh yeshiva*, and chair in Jewish thought at Mechon Hadar in New York, New York.

Hayim Herring, rabbi, is CEO of Herring Consulting Network.

Abraham Joshua Heschel (1907–1972) was a Polish-born, American Jewish theologian and rabbi who taught at The Jewish Theological Seminary of America.

Lawrence A. Hoffman has served for more than three decades as professor of liturgy at Hebrew Union College–Jewish Institute of Religion in New York. He is a world-renowned liturgist and holder of the Stephen and Barbara Friedman Chair in Liturgy, Worship and Ritual.

David A. Ingber is rabbi of Romemu in New York, New York.

Ben Kamin is a rabbi and author who formerly led The Temple–Tifereth Israel in Cleveland, Ohio.

Yehuda Karni (1884–1949) was a Hebrew poet from Minsk who eventually settled in Israel and was on the editorial board of *Haaretz* until his death.

Paul J. Kipnes is rabbi of Or Ami in Calabasas, California.

Eliahu J. Klein is a Jewish chaplain for the State of California.

Jeffrey Klepper serves as cantor of Temple Sinai in Sharon, Massachusetts.

Michael Knopf is a rabbi at Har Zion Temple in Philadelphia, Pennsylvania.

Harold Kohn is a member of the faculty of the University of North Carolina School of Pharmacy.

Abraham Isaac Kook (1865–1935), mystic and kabbalist, served as the first chief rabbi of Israel.

Andy Koren is rabbi at Temple Emanuel in Greensboro, North Carolina.

Cary Kozberg is rabbi of the Wexner Heritage House in Columbus, Ohio.

Elliot Kukla is a rabbi at the Bay Area Jewish Healing Center in San Francisco, California.

Irwin Kula, rabbi, is copresident of Clal—The National Jewish Center for Learning and Leadership.

Harold S. Kushner is rabbi laureate of Temple Israel of Natick in Natick, Massachusetts.

Lawrence Kushner, rabbi, serves as scholar-in-residence of Temple Emanu-El in San Francisco, California.

Robert N. Levine is rabbi of Rodeph Shalom Congregation in New York, New York.

Levi Yitzchak of Berditchev (1740–1809), rabbi, was well known for his posture called *chutzpah k'lappei malah* (chutzpah in the face of heaven), which challenged God.

Stan Levy is founder, rabbi, and spiritual leader of B'nai Horin— Children of Freedom in Los Angeles, California.

Immanuel Lubliner (1923–1997) served as rabbi of Greenburgh Jewish Center in Dobbs Ferry, New York.

Moses Maimonides (1135–1204) was a rabbi, theologian, and physician, in Moorish Spain and then in Egypt, and is considered by many as the greatest medieval Jewish philosopher.

Mar the son of Rabina (fourth century) was a Talmudic Rabbi.

Craig Marantz is rabbi of Congregation Kol Haverim in Gastonbury, Connecticut.

Danny Maseng is a singer songwriter, and *chazzan* of Temple Israel in Hollywood, California.

Daniel C. Matt is a scholar and translator of the central book of Jewish mysticism, the *Zohar*.

Hershel Jonah Matt (1922–1987) served as rabbi of several congregations, the last of which was the Princeton Jewish Center in New Jersey.

Ralph D. Mecklenburger is rabbi of Beth El Congregation in Fort Worth, Texas.

Andrew Meit is a graphic artist and programmer.

Joseph B. Meszler is rabbi of Temple Sinai in Sharon, Massachusetts.

Jay Michaelson, writer and thinker, is founder of Nehirim: GLBT Jewish Culture and Spirituality and of the online magazine, *Zeek: A Jewish Journal of Thought and Culture*.

James L. Mirel is rabbi of Temple B'nai Torah in Bellevue, Washington.

Nachman of Breslov (1772–1810) was founder of the Breslov Hasidic movement, known for its spiritual approach to Judaism.

Louis Newman is director of faculty development, Judaic studies, the Perlman Center for Learning and Teaching. He is the Humphrey Doermann Professor of Liberal Learning and John M. and Elizabeth W. Musser Professor of Religious Studies at Carleton College in Northfield, Minnesota.

Dan Nichols is a singer and songwriter.

Reb Noson (1780–1844) was the primary disciple and scribe of Rabbi Nachman of Breslov.

Avi S. Olitzky is a rabbi at Beth El Synagogue in St. Louis Park, Minnesota.

Jesse Olitzky is a rabbi at the Jacksonville Jewish Center in Jacksonville, Florida.

Kerry M. Olitzky is a rabbi who serves as executive director of the Jewish Outreach Institute.

Natan Ophir (Offenbacher) teaches Jewish thought at the Hebrew University of Jerusalem.

Bachya ibn Pakuda (eleventh century) was a Spanish philosopher and rabbi.

Daniel F. Polish serves as spiritual leader of Congregation Shir Chadash of the Hudson Valley in Poughkeepsie, New York.

Andrew Ramer is author of several books, including *Ask Your Angel*.

Avrom Reyzen (1876–1953) was a Yiddish writer, poet, and editor.

Haim O. Rechnitzer teaches modern Jewish thought at Hebrew Union College–Jewish Institute of Religion, Cincinnati, Ohio.

Jack Riemer is rabbi of Congregation Beth Tikvah in Boca Raton, Florida.

Albert Ringer is rabbi of the Reform community of Rotterdam, the Netherlands and chaplain in the Dutch army.

Brant Rosen is rabbi of Jewish Reconstructionist Congregation in Evanston, Illinois.

James B. Rosenberg is rabbi emeritus of Temple Habonim in Cranston, Rhode Island.

Joel Rosenberg is a poet, translator, and writer.

Robert Saks is rabbi emeritus of Congregation Bet Mishpachah in Washington, D.C.

Jeffrey Salkin is a rabbi who serves as the director of the New Jersey region of the Anti-Defamation League (ADL).

Neil Sandler is senior rabbi at Ahavath Achim Synagogue in Atlanta, Georgia.

Zalman Schachter-Shalomi, rabbi, is considered to be the founder of the Jewish Renewal Movement.

Robert Scheinberg is rabbi of the United Synagogue in Hoboken, New Jersey.

Harold M. Schulweis is rabbi of Temple Valley Beth Shalom in Encino, California.

Arthur Segal is a rabbi who specializes in Jewish spiritual renewal.

Allen Selis is headmaster of South Peninsula Hebrew Day School in Palo Alto, California.

Rami M. Shapiro, rabbi, is an award-winning poet and author.

Andrew Shaw is executive director of Tribe and community development rabbi of Stanmore United Synagogue in the United Kingdom.

Rick Sherwin is rabbi of Congregation Beth Am in Longwood, Florida.

Shneur Zalman of Liadi (1745–1812) was the founder of Chabad Hasidism and author of the *Tanya*.

Yaakov David Shulman is a writer, translator, and editor.

Danny Siegel is a poet whose work in *tzedakah* (charitable giving) is renown.

Rifat Sonsino is rabbi emeritus of Temple Beth Shalom in Needham, Massachusetts, and adjunct professor of theology at Boston College.

Wally "Velvel" Spiegler lives in Massachusetts.

Elie Kaplan Spitz is rabbi of Congregation B'nai Israel in Tustin, California.

Chaim Stern (1930–2001) served as rabbi of Temple Beth El in Chappaqua, New York.

Arnold Stiebel, rabbi, is a family and pastoral counselor at Meditation Matters in Woodland Hills, California.

Warren Stone is rabbi of Temple Emanuel in Kensington, Maryland.

Neil A. Tow is rabbi of the Glen Rock Jewish Center in Glen Rock, New Jersey.

Roy A. Walter is rabbi emeritus of Temple Emanuel in Houston, Texas.

Simkha Y. Weintraub serves as the rabbinic director of the Jewish Board of Children and Family Services in New York, New York.

David Wolpe is rabbi of Sinai Temple in Los Angeles, California.

Hillel Zeitlin (1871–1942) was a Yiddish and Hebrew writer who edited the Yiddish newspaper *Moment*.

Reuben Zellman is rabbi and music director at Congregation Beth El in Berkeley, California.

Daniel G. Zemel is rabbi of Temple Micah in Washington, D.C.

Shawn Zevit is a Reconstructionist rabbi, singer, and songwriter whose work has focused on outreach to congregations and the men's movement in Judaism.

Sheldon Zimmerman is rabbi of the Jewish Center of the Hamptons in East Hampton, New York.

Mishael Zion, rabbi, is codirector of Bronfman Youth Fellowships.

Raymond A. Zwerin is founding rabbi of Temple Sinai in Denver, Colorado.

Credits

Jewish Lights is grateful to the following authors and publishers for permission to reproduce the material listed below. These pages constitute a continuation of the copyright page. Every effort has been made to trace and acknowledge copyright holders of all the material included in this anthology. The editors apologize for any errors or omissions that may remain and ask that any omissions be brought to their attention so that they may be corrected in future editions. Please send corrections to:

Editors at Jewish Lights Publishing
c/o Jewish Lights Publishing
Sunset Farm Offices Route 4, P.O. Box 237
Woodstock, VT 05091

Israel Abrahams, "Finding You," from *The Standard Book of Jewish Verse*, George Alexander Kohut, ed.

Reb Aharon of Karlin, "*Yah Ekhsof Noam Shabbat*," trans. by Rabbi Zalman Schachter-Shalomi. © 2013 Zalman Schachter-Shalomi.

Rabbi Daniel S. Alexander, "After Psalm 16," © 2012 by Daniel S. Alexander.

Rabbi Alexandri, "Following the *Amidah*," from Babylonian Talmud, *Berakhot* 17a.

"*Tefillah*." Courtesy Bezalel Aloni, the songwriter-producer-manager of the late legendary singer Ofra Haza.

Rabbi Bradley Shavit Artson, "A *Yizkor* Blessing"; "An Insertion into the *Amidah* for Autism"; and "Prayer for a Mourner." © 2013 by Bradley Shavit Artson.

Rebbe Eilmelech of Lizhensk, "A Prayer for Friendship," trans. from Natan Ophir (Offenbacher), *Rabbi Shlomo Carlebach: Life, Mission, and Legacy*. Urim Publications: Jerusalem-New York © 2013.

Rabbi Elimelech of Lizhensk, "That We May Pray Well," quoted passage from Psalm 25:7 trans. by Rabbi Zalman Schachter-Shalomi. © 2013 by Zalman Schachter-Shalomi.

Rabbi Dov Peretz Elkins, "Prayer for the New Year." © 2013 by Dov Peretz Elkins.

Abraham ibn Ezra, "I See You," from *Reflections and Readings for the High Holy Days*, comp. by Marc. H. Wilson. © 1989 by Temple Israel (Charlotte, NC: Temple Israel).

Rabbi Morley T. Feinstein, "The Hour of Remembrance." © 2013 by Morley T. Feinstein.

Rabbi Edward Feld, "Psalm 93: An Interpretive Translation," from *Mahzor Lev Shalem*, ed. by Edward Feld. © 2010 by The Rabbinical Assembly (New York: The Rabbinical Assembly).

Rabbi Mordecai Finley, "May God Protect You." © 2013 by Mordecai Finley.

Rabbi Adam D. Fisher, "Blessings of Pleasure," from *Seder Tu Bishevat: The Festival of Trees*. © 1989 by CCAR Press.

Rabbi Adam D. Fisher, "God Dwells Wherever We Let Him In" and "O Lord." © 2013 by Adam D. Fisher.

Rabbi Ira Flax, "A Prayer following the Fifteen Morning Benedictions." © 2013 by Ira Flax.

Solomon ibn Gabirol, "At Dawn I Seek You." © 2013 by Solomon ibn Gabirol.

Rabbi Elihu Gevirtz, "A Prayer for My Subconscious in Response to the Rebbe's Torah," based on Rebbe Nachman of Breslov's *Likutey Moharan, Chelek 2*, lesson 5:14; "Come Close: A Prayer"; "Meditation Face to Face"; and "Meditation on the *Tikkun* of Food," based on Rebbe Nachman of Breslov's *Likutey Moharan, Chelek 2*, lesson 1:4. © 2013 by Elihu Gevirtz.

Rabbi Zalman Goldstein, "Pardon Me, Forgive Me," from *The Jewish Mourner's Companion*. © 2006.

Index of Contributors

Index of First Lines

Congregation Resources

Jewish Megatrends: Charting the Course of the American Jewish Future
By Rabbi Sidney Schwarz; Foreword by Ambassador Stuart E. Eizenstat
Visionary solutions for a community ripe for transformational change—from fourteen leading innovators of Jewish life.
6 x 9, 288 pp, HC, 978-1-58023-667-6 **$24.99**

Relational Judaism: Using the Power of Relationships to Transform the Jewish Community *By Dr. Ron Wolfson*
How to transform the model of twentieth-century Jewish institutions into twenty-first-century relational communities offering meaning and purpose, belonging and blessing.
6 x 9, 288 pp, HC, 978-1-58023-666-9 **$24.99**

Revolution of Jewish Spirit: How to Revive *Ruakh* in Your Spiritual Life, Transform Your Synagogue & Inspire Your Jewish Community
By Rabbi Baruch HaLevi, DMin, and Ellen Frankel, LCSW; Foreword by Dr. Ron Wolfson
A practical and engaging guide to reinvigorating Jewish life. Offers strategies for sustaining and expanding transformation, impassioned leadership, inspired programming and inviting sacred spaces.
6 x 9, 224 pp, Quality PB Original, 978-1-58023-625-6 **$19.99**

Building a Successful Volunteer Culture: Finding Meaning in Service in the Jewish Community *By Rabbi Charles Simon; Foreword by Shelley Lindauer; Preface by Dr. Ron Wolfson*
6 x 9, 192 pp, Quality PB, 978-1-58023-408-5 **$16.99**

The Case for Jewish Peoplehood: Can We Be One?
By Dr. Erica Brown and Dr. Misha Galperin; Foreword by Rabbi Joseph Telushkin
6 x 9, 224 pp, HC, 978-1-58023-401-6 **$21.99**

Empowered Judaism: What Independent Minyanim Can Teach Us about Building Vibrant Jewish Communities *By Rabbi Elie Kaunfer; Foreword by Prof. Jonathan D. Sarna*
6 x 9, 224 pp, Quality PB, 978-1-58023-412-2 **$18.99**

Finding a Spiritual Home: How a New Generation of Jews Can Transform the American Synagogue *By Rabbi Sidney Schwarz*
6 x 9, 352 pp, Quality PB, 978-1-58023-185-5 **$19.95**

Inspired Jewish Leadership: Practical Approaches to Building Strong Communities
By Dr. Erica Brown 6 x 9, 256 pp, HC, 978-1-58023-361-3 **$27.99**

Jewish Pastoral Care, 2nd Edition: A Practical Handbook from Traditional & Contemporary Sources *Edited by Rabbi Dayle A. Friedman, MSW, MAJCS, BCC*
6 x 9, 528 pp, Quality PB, 978-1-58023-427-6 **$35.00**

Jewish Spiritual Direction: An Innovative Guide from Traditional and Contemporary Sources
Edited by Rabbi Howard A. Addison, PhD, and Barbara Eve Breitman, MSW
6 x 9, 368 pp, HC, 978-1-58023-230-2 **$30.00**

A Practical Guide to Rabbinic Counseling
Edited by Rabbi Yisrael N. Levitz, PhD, and Rabbi Abraham J. Twerski, MD
6 x 9, 432 pp, HC, 978-1-58023-562-4 **$40.00**

Professional Spiritual & Pastoral Care: A Practical Clergy and Chaplain's Handbook
Edited by Rabbi Stephen B. Roberts, MBA, MHL, BCJC
6 x 9, 480 pp, HC, 978-1-59473-312-3 **$50.00**

Reimagining Leadership in Jewish Organizations: Ten Practical Lessons to Help You Implement Change and Achieve Your Goals *By Dr. Misha Galperin*
6 x 9, 192 pp, Quality PB, 978-1-58023-492-4 **$16.99**

Rethinking Synagogues: A New Vocabulary for Congregational Life
By Rabbi Lawrence A. Hoffman, PhD 6 x 9, 240 pp, Quality PB, 978-1-58023-248-7 **$19.99**

Spiritual Community: The Power to Restore Hope, Commitment and Joy
By Rabbi David A. Teutsch, PhD
5½ x 8½, 144 pp, HC, 978-1-58023-270-8 **$19.99**

Spiritual Boredom: Rediscovering the Wonder of Judaism *By Dr. Erica Brown*
6 x 9, 208 pp, HC, 978-1-58023-405-4 **$21.99**

The Spirituality of Welcoming: How to Transform Your Congregation into a Sacred Community *By Dr. Ron Wolfson* 6 x 9, 224 pp, Quality PB, 978-1-58023-244-9 **$19.99**

Ecology / Environment

A Wild Faith: Jewish Ways into Wilderness, Wilderness Ways into Judaism
By Rabbi Mike Comins; Foreword by Nigel Savage 6 x 9, 240 pp, Quality PB, 978-1-58023-316-3 **$16.99**

Ecology & the Jewish Spirit: Where Nature & the Sacred Meet
Edited by Ellen Bernstein 6 x 9, 288 pp, Quality PB, 978-1-58023-082-7 **$18.99**

Torah of the Earth: Exploring 4,000 Years of Ecology in Jewish Thought
Vol. 1: Biblical Israel & Rabbinic Judaism; Vol. 2: Zionism & Eco-Judaism
Edited by Rabbi Arthur Waskow Vol. 1: 6 x 9, 272 pp, Quality PB, 978-1-58023-086-5 **$19.95**
Vol. 2: 6 x 9, 336 pp, Quality PB, 978-1-58023-087-2 **$19.95**

The Way Into Judaism and the Environment *By Jeremy Benstein, PhD*
6 x 9, 288 pp, Quality PB, 978-1-58023-368-2 **$18.99**; HC, 978-1-58023-268-5 **$24.99**

Graphic Novels / Graphic History

The Adventures of Rabbi Harvey: A Graphic Novel of Jewish Wisdom and Wit in the
Wild West *By Steve Sheinkin* 6 x 9, 144 pp, Full-color illus., Quality PB, 978-1-58023-310-1 **$16.99**

Rabbi Harvey Rides Again: A Graphic Novel of Jewish Folktales Let Loose in the
Wild West *By Steve Sheinkin* 6 x 9, 144 pp, Full-color illus., Quality PB, 978-1-58023-347-7 **$16.99**

Rabbi Harvey vs. the Wisdom Kid: A Graphic Novel of Dueling
Jewish Folktales in the Wild West *By Steve Sheinkin*
Rabbi Harvey's first book-length adventure—and toughest challenge.
6 x 9, 144 pp, Full-color illus., Quality PB, 978-1-58023-422-1 **$16.99**

The Story of the Jews: A 4,000-Year Adventure—A Graphic History Book
By Stan Mack 6 x 9, 288 pp, Illus., Quality PB, 978-1-58023-155-8 **$16.99**

Grief / Healing

Facing Illness, Finding God: How Judaism Can Help You and
Caregivers Cope When Body or Spirit Fails *By Rabbi Joseph B. Meszler*
Will help you find spiritual strength for healing amid the fear, pain and chaos of
illness. 6 x 9, 208 pp, Quality PB, 978-1-58023-423-8 **$16.99**

Midrash & Medicine: Healing Body and Soul in the Jewish Interpretive
Tradition *Edited by Rabbi William Cutter, PhD; Foreword by Michele F. Prince, LCSW, MAJCS*
Explores how midrash can help you see beyond the physical aspects of healing to
tune in to your spiritual source.
6 x 9, 352 pp, Quality PB, 978-1-58023-484-9 **$21.99**

Healing from Despair: Choosing Wholeness in a Broken World
By Rabbi Elie Kaplan Spitz with Erica Shapiro Taylor; Foreword by Abraham J. Twerski, MD
5½ x 8½, 208 pp, Quality PB, 978-1-58023-436-8 **$16.99**

Healing and the Jewish Imagination: Spiritual and Practical Perspectives on
Judaism and Health *Edited by Rabbi William Cutter, PhD*
6 x 9, 240 pp, Quality PB, 978-1-58023-373-6 **$19.99**

Grief in Our Seasons: A Mourner's Kaddish Companion *By Rabbi Kerry M. Olitzky*
4½ x 6½, 448 pp, Quality PB, 978-1-879045-55-2 **$15.95**

Healing of Soul, Healing of Body: Spiritual Leaders Unfold the Strength & Solace
in Psalms *Edited by Rabbi Simkha Y. Weintraub, LCSW*
6 x 9, 128 pp, 2-color illus. text, Quality PB, 978-1-879045-31-6 **$16.99**

Mourning & Mitzvah, 2nd Edition: A Guided Journal for Walking the Mourner's
Path through Grief to Healing *By Rabbi Anne Brener, LCSW*
7½ x 9, 304 pp, Quality PB, 978-1-58023-113-8 **$19.99**

Tears of Sorrow, Seeds of Hope, 2nd Edition: A Jewish Spiritual Companion
for Infertility and Pregnancy Loss *By Rabbi Nina Beth Cardin*
6 x 9, 208 pp, Quality PB, 978-1-58023-233-3 **$18.99**

A Time to Mourn, a Time to Comfort, 2nd Edition: A Guide to Jewish
Bereavement *By Dr. Ron Wolfson; Foreword by Rabbi David J. Wolpe*
7 x 9, 384 pp, Quality PB, 978-1-58023-253-1 **$21.99**

When a Grandparent Dies: A Kid's Own Remembering Workbook for Dealing
with Shiva and the Year Beyond *By Nechama Liss-Levinson, PhD*
8 x 10, 48 pp, 2-color text, HC, 978-1-879045-44-6 **$15.95** For ages 7–13

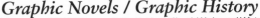

Social Justice

Where Justice Dwells
A Hands-On Guide to Doing Social Justice in Your Jewish Community
By Rabbi Jill Jacobs; Foreword by Rabbi David Saperstein
Provides ways to envision and act on your own ideals of social justice.
7 x 9, 288 pp, Quality PB Original, 978-1-58023-453-5 **$24.99**

There Shall Be No Needy
Pursuing Social Justice through Jewish Law and Tradition
By Rabbi Jill Jacobs; Foreword by Rabbi Elliot N. Dorff, PhD; Preface by Simon Greer
Confronts the most pressing issues of twenty-first-century America from a deeply Jewish perspective. 6 x 9, 288 pp, Quality PB, 978-1-58023-425-2 **$16.99**
There Shall Be No Needy Teacher's Guide 8½ x 11, 56 pp, PB, 978-1-58023-429-0 **$8.99**

Conscience
The Duty to Obey and the Duty to Disobey
By Rabbi Harold M. Schulweis
Examines the idea of conscience and the role conscience plays in our relationships to government, law, ethics, religion, human nature, God—and to each other.
6 x 9, 160 pp, Quality PB, 978-1-58023-419-1 **$16.99**; HC, 978-1-58023-375-0 **$19.99**

Judaism and Justice
The Jewish Passion to Repair the World
By Rabbi Sidney Schwarz; Foreword by Ruth Messinger
Explores the relationship between Judaism, social justice and the Jewish identity of American Jews. 6 x 9, 352 pp, Quality PB, 978-1-58023-353-8 **$19.99**

Travel

Israel—A Spiritual Travel Guide, 2nd Edition: A Companion for the Modern Jewish Pilgrim *By Rabbi Lawrence A. Hoffman, PhD*
Helps today's pilgrim tap into the deep spiritual meaning of the ancient—and modern—sites of the Holy Land.
4¾ x 10, 256 pp, Illus., Quality PB, 978-1-58023-261-6 **$18.99**
Also Available: **The Israel Mission Leader's Guide** 5½ x 8½, 16 pp, PB, 978-1-58023-085-8 **$4.95**

Twelve Steps

Recovery—The Sacred Art: The Twelve Steps as Spiritual Practice
By Rami Shapiro; Foreword by Joan Borysenko, PhD
Draws on insights and practices of different religious traditions to help you move more deeply into the universal spirituality of the Twelve Step system.
5½ x 8½, 240 pp, Quality PB Original, 978-1-59473-259-1 **$16.99**
(A book from SkyLight Paths, Jewish Lights' sister imprint)

100 Blessings Every Day: Daily Twelve Step Recovery Affirmations, Exercises for Personal Growth & Renewal Reflecting Seasons of the Jewish Year *By Rabbi Kerry M. Olitzky; Foreword by Rabbi Neil Gillman, PhD* 4½ x 6½, 432 pp, Quality PB, 978-1-879045-30-9 **$16.99**

Recovery from Codependence: A Jewish Twelve Steps Guide to Healing Your Soul
By Rabbi Kerry M. Olitzky 6 x 9, 160 pp, Quality PB, 978-1-879045-32-3 **$13.95**

Twelve Jewish Steps to Recovery, 2nd Edition: A Personal Guide to Turning from Alcoholism & Other Addictions—Drugs, Food, Gambling, Sex...
By Rabbi Kerry M. Olitzky and Stuart A. Copans, MD; Preface by Abraham J. Twerski, MD
6 x 9, 160 pp, Quality PB, 978-1-58023-409-2 **$16.99**

Holidays / Holy Days

Prayers of Awe Series

An exciting new series that examines the High Holy Day liturgy to enrich the praying experience of everyone—whether experienced worshipers or guests who encounter Jewish prayer for the very first time.

We Have Sinned—Sin and Confession in Judaism: *Ashamnu* and *Al Chet*
Edited by Rabbi Lawrence A. Hoffman, PhD
A varied and fascinating look at sin, confession and pardon in Judaism, as suggested by the centrality of *Ashamnu* and *Al Chet*, two prayers that people know so well, though understand so little. 6 x 9, 304 pp, HC, 978-1-58023-612-6 **$24.99**

Who by Fire, Who by Water—*Un'taneh Tokef*
Edited by Rabbi Lawrence A. Hoffman, PhD 6 x 9, 272 pp, HC, 978-1-58023-424-5 **$24.99**

All These Vows—*Kol Nidre*
Edited by Rabbi Lawrence A. Hoffman, PhD 6 x 9, 288 pp, HC, 978-1-58023-430-6 **$24.99**

Rosh Hashanah Readings: Inspiration, Information and Contemplation
Yom Kippur Readings: Inspiration, Information and Contemplation
Edited by Rabbi Dov Peretz Elkins; Section Introductions from Arthur Green's These Are the Words
Rosh Hashanah: 6 x 9, 400 pp, Quality PB, 978-1-58023-437-5 **$19.99**
Yom Kippur: 6 x 9, 368 pp, Quality PB, 978-1-58023-438-2 **$19.99**; HC, 978-1-58023-271-5 **$24.99**

Reclaiming Judaism as a Spiritual Practice: Holy Days and Shabbat
By Rabbi Goldie Milgram 7 x 9, 272 pp, Quality PB, 978-1-58023-205-0 **$19.99**

The Sabbath Soul: Mystical Reflections on the Transformative Power of Holy Time
Selection, Translation and Commentary by Eitan Fishbane, PhD
6 x 9, 208 pp, Quality PB, 978-1-58023-459-7 **$18.99**

Shabbat, 2nd Edition: The Family Guide to Preparing for and Celebrating the Sabbath
By Dr. Ron Wolfson 7 x 9, 320 pp, Illus., Quality PB, 978-1-58023-164-0 **$19.99**

Hanukkah, 2nd Edition: The Family Guide to Spiritual Celebration
By Dr. Ron Wolfson 7 x 9, 240 pp, Illus., Quality PB, 978-1-58023-122-0 **$18.95**

Passover

My People's Passover Haggadah
Traditional Texts, Modern Commentaries
Edited by Rabbi Lawrence A. Hoffman, PhD, and David Arnow, PhD
A diverse and exciting collection of commentaries on the traditional Passover Haggadah—in two volumes!
Vol. 1: 7 x 10, 304 pp, HC, 978-1-58023-354-5 **$24.99**
Vol. 2: 7 x 10, 320 pp, HC, 978-1-58023-346-0 **$24.99**

Freedom Journeys: The Tale of Exodus and Wilderness across Millennia
By Rabbi Arthur O. Waskow and Rabbi Phyllis O. Berman
Explores how the story of Exodus echoes in our own time, calling us to relearn and rethink the Passover story through social-justice, ecological, feminist and interfaith perspectives. 6 x 9, 288 pp, HC, 978-1-58023-445-0 **$24.99**

Leading the Passover Journey: The Seder's Meaning Revealed,
the Haggadah's Story Retold *By Rabbi Nathan Laufer*
Uncovers the hidden meaning of the Seder's rituals and customs.
6 x 9, 224 pp, Quality PB, 978-1-58023-399-6 **$18.99**

Creating Lively Passover Seders, 2nd Edition: A Sourcebook of Engaging Tales,
Texts & Activities *By David Arnow, PhD* 7 x 9, 464 pp, Quality PB, 978-1-58023-444-3 **$24.99**

Passover, 2nd Edition: The Family Guide to Spiritual Celebration
By Dr. Ron Wolfson with Joel Lurie Grishaver 7 x 9, 416 pp, Quality PB, 978-1-58023-174-5 **$19.95**

The Women's Passover Companion: Women's Reflections on the Festival of Freedom
Edited by Rabbi Sharon Cohen Anisfeld, Tara Mohr and Catherine Spector; Foreword by Paula E. Hyman
6 x 9, 352 pp, Quality PB, 978-1-58023-231-9 **$19.99**; HC, 978-1-58023-128-2 **$24.95**

The Women's Seder Sourcebook: Rituals & Readings for Use at the Passover Seder
Edited by Rabbi Sharon Cohen Anisfeld, Tara Mohr and Catherine Spector
6 x 9, 384 pp, Quality PB, 978-1-58023-232-6 **$19.99**

Theology / Philosophy / The Way Into... Series

The Way Into... series offers an accessible and highly usable "guided tour" of the Jewish faith, people, history and beliefs—in total, an introduction to Judaism that will enable you to understand and interact with the sacred texts of the Jewish tradition. Each volume is written by a leading contemporary scholar and teacher, and explores one key aspect of Judaism. The Way Into... series enables all readers to achieve a real sense of Jewish cultural literacy through guided study.

The Way Into Encountering God in Judaism
By Rabbi Neil Gillman, PhD

For everyone who wants to understand how Jews have encountered God throughout history and today.

6 x 9, 240 pp, Quality PB, 978-1-58023-199-2 **$18.99**; HC, 978-1-58023-025-4 **$21.95**

Also Available: **The Jewish Approach to God:** A Brief Introduction for Christians
By Rabbi Neil Gillman, PhD

5½ x 8½, 192 pp, Quality PB, 978-1-58023-190-9 **$16.95**

The Way Into Jewish Mystical Tradition
By Rabbi Lawrence Kushner

Allows readers to interact directly with the sacred mystical texts of the Jewish tradition. An accessible introduction to the concepts of Jewish mysticism, their religious and spiritual significance, and how they relate to life today.

6 x 9, 224 pp, Quality PB, 978-1-58023-200-5 **$18.99**; HC, 978-1-58023-029-2 **$21.95**

The Way Into Jewish Prayer
By Rabbi Lawrence A. Hoffman, PhD

Opens the door to 3,000 years of Jewish prayer, making anyone feel at home in the Jewish way of communicating with God.

6 x 9, 208 pp, Quality PB, 978-1-58023-201-2 **$18.99**

The Way Into Jewish Prayer Teacher's Guide
By Rabbi Jennifer Ossakow Goldsmith

8½ x 11, 42 pp, PB, 978-1-58023-345-3 **$8.99**

Download a free copy at www.jewishlights.com.

The Way Into Judaism and the Environment
By Jeremy Benstein, PhD

Explores the ways in which Judaism contributes to contemporary social-environmental issues, the extent to which Judaism is part of the problem and how it can be part of the solution.

6 x 9, 288 pp, Quality PB, 978-1-58023-368-2 **$18.99**; HC, 978-1-58023-268-5 **$24.99**

The Way Into Tikkun Olam (Repairing the World)
By Rabbi Elliot N. Dorff, PhD

An accessible introduction to the Jewish concept of the individual's responsibility to care for others and repair the world.

6 x 9, 304 pp, Quality PB, 978-1-58023-328-6 **$18.99**

The Way Into Torah
By Rabbi Norman J. Cohen, PhD

Helps guide you in the exploration of the origins and development of Torah, explains why it should be studied and how to do it.

6 x 9, 176 pp, Quality PB, 978-1-58023-198-5 **$16.99**

The Way Into the Varieties of Jewishness
By Sylvia Barack Fishman, PhD

Explores the religious and historical understanding of what it has meant to be Jewish from ancient times to the present controversy over "Who is a Jew?"

6 x 9, 288 pp, Quality PB, 978-1-58023-367-5 **$18.99**; HC, 978-1-58023-030-8 **$24.99**

Theology / Philosophy

From Defender to Critic: The Search for a New Jewish Self
By Dr. David Hartman
A daring self-examination of Hartman's goals, which were not to strip halakha of
its authority but to create a space for questioning and critique that allows for the
traditionally religious Jew to act out a moral life in tune with modern experience.
6 x 9, 336 pp, HC, 978-1-58023-515-0 **$35.00**

Our Religious Brains: What Cognitive Science Reveals about Belief,
Morality, Community and Our Relationship with God
By Rabbi Ralph D. Mecklenburger; Foreword by Dr. Howard Kelfer; Preface by Dr. Neil Gillman
This is a groundbreaking, accessible look at the implications of cognitive science for
religion and theology, intended for laypeople. 6 x 9, 224 pp, HC, 978-1-58023-508-2 **$24.99**

The Other Talmud—The Yerushalmi: Unlocking the Secrets of The
Talmud of Israel for Judaism Today *By Rabbi Judith Z. Abrams, PhD*
A fascinating—and stimulating—look at "the other Talmud" and the possibilities
for Jewish life reflected there. 6 x 9, 256 pp, HC, 978-1-58023-463-4 **$24.99**

The Way of Man: According to Hasidic Teaching
*By Martin Buber; New Translation and Introduction by Rabbi Bernard H. Mehlman and Dr.
Gabriel E. Padawer; Foreword by Paul Mendes-Flohr*
An accessible and engaging new translation of Buber's classic work—available as
an e-book only. E-book, 978-1-58023-601-0 Digital List Price **$14.99**

The Death of Death: Resurrection and Immortality in Jewish Thought
By Rabbi Neil Gillman, PhD 6 x 9, 336 pp, Quality PB, 978-1-58023-081-0 **$18.95**

Doing Jewish Theology: God, Torah & Israel in Modern Judaism *By Rabbi Neil Gillman, PhD*
6 x 9, 304 pp, Quality PB, 978-1-58023-439-9 **$18.99**; HC, 978-1-58023-322-4 **$24.99**

A Heart of Many Rooms: Celebrating the Many Voices within Judaism
By Dr. David Hartman 6 x 9, 352 pp, Quality PB, 978-1-58023-156-5 **$19.95**

The God Who Hates Lies: Confronting & Rethinking Jewish Tradition
By Dr. David Hartman with Charlie Buckholtz 6 x 9, 208 pp, HC, 978-1-58023-455-9 **$24.99**

Jewish Theology in Our Time: A New Generation Explores the Foundations and
Future of Jewish Belief *Edited by Rabbi Elliot J. Cosgrove, PhD; Foreword by Rabbi David J. Wolpe;
Preface by Rabbi Carole B. Balin, PhD* 6 x 9, 240 pp, HC, 978-1-58023-413-9 **$24.99**

Maimonides—Essential Teachings on Jewish Faith & Ethics: The Book of
Knowledge & the Thirteen Principles of Faith—Annotated & Explained
Translation and Annotation by Rabbi Marc D. Angel, PhD
5½ x 8½, 224 pp, Quality PB Original, 978-1-59473-311-6 **$18.99***

Maimonides, Spinoza and Us: Toward an Intellectually Vibrant Judaism
By Rabbi Marc D. Angel, PhD 6 x 9, 224 pp, HC, 978-1-58023-411-5 **$24.99**

A Touch of the Sacred: A Theologian's Informal Guide to Jewish Belief
By Dr. Eugene B. Borowitz and Frances W. Schwartz
6 x 9, 256 pp, Quality PB, 978-1-58023-416-0 **$16.99**; HC, 978-1-58023-337-8 **$21.99**

Traces of God: Seeing God in Torah, History and Everyday Life *By Rabbi Neil Gillman, PhD*
6 x 9, 240 pp, Quality PB, 978-1-58023-369-9 **$16.99**

Your Word Is Fire: The Hasidic Masters on Contemplative Prayer
Edited and translated by Rabbi Arthur Green, PhD, and Barry W. Holtz
6 x 9, 160 pp, Quality PB, 978-1-879045-25-5 **$16.99**

I Am Jewish
Personal Reflections Inspired by the Last Words of Daniel Pearl
Almost 150 Jews—both famous and not—from all walks of life, from all around
the world, write about many aspects of their Judaism.
    Edited by Judea and Ruth Pearl 6 x 9, 304 pp, Deluxe PB w/ flaps, 978-1-58023-259-3 **$18.99**
Download a free copy of the *I Am Jewish Teacher's Guide* at www.jewishlights.com.
Hannah Senesh: Her Life and Diary, The First Complete Edition
    By Hannah Senesh; Foreword by Marge Piercy; Preface by Eitan Senesh; Afterword by Roberta Grossman
6 x 9, 368 pp, b/w photos, Quality PB, 978-1-58023-342-2 **$19.99**

*A book from SkyLight Paths, Jewish Lights' sister imprint

Meditation

Jewish Meditation Practices for Everyday Life
Awakening Your Heart, Connecting with God
By Rabbi Jeff Roth
Offers a fresh take on meditation that draws on life experience and living life with greater clarity as opposed to the traditional method of rigorous study.
6 x 9, 224 pp, Quality PB, 978-1-58023-397-2 **$18.99**

The Handbook of Jewish Meditation Practices
A Guide for Enriching the Sabbath and Other Days of Your Life
By Rabbi David A. Cooper Easy-to-learn meditation techniques.
6 x 9, 208 pp, Quality PB, 978-1-58023-102-1 **$16.95**

Discovering Jewish Meditation, 2nd Edition
Instruction & Guidance for Learning an Ancient Spiritual Practice
By Nan Fink Gefen, PhD 6 x 9, 208 pp, Quality PB, 978-1-58023-462-7 **$16.99**

Meditation from the Heart of Judaism
Today's Teachers Share Their Practices, Techniques, and Faith
Edited by Avram Davis 6 x 9, 256 pp, Quality PB, 978-1-58023-049-0 **$16.95**

Ritual / Sacred Practices

The Jewish Dream Book: The Key to Opening the Inner Meaning of Your Dreams
By Vanessa L. Ochs, PhD, with Elizabeth Ochs; Illus. by Kristina Swarner
Instructions for how modern people can perform ancient Jewish dream practices and dream interpretations drawn from the Jewish wisdom tradition.
8 x 8, 128 pp, Full-color illus., Deluxe PB w/ flaps, 978-1-58023-132-9 **$16.95**

God in Your Body: Kabbalah, Mindfulness and Embodied Spiritual Practice
By Jay Michaelson
The first comprehensive treatment of the body in Jewish spiritual practice and an essential guide to the sacred.
6 x 9, 272 pp, Quality PB, 978-1-58023-304-0 **$18.99**

The Book of Jewish Sacred Practices: CLAL's Guide to Everyday & Holiday Rituals & Blessings
Edited by Rabbi Irwin Kula and Vanessa L. Ochs, PhD
6 x 9, 368 pp, Quality PB, 978-1-58023-152-7 **$18.95**

Jewish Ritual: A Brief Introduction for Christians
By Rabbi Kerry M. Olitzky and Rabbi Daniel Judson
5½ x 8½, 144 pp, Quality PB, 978-1-58023-210-4 **$14.99**

The Rituals & Practices of a Jewish Life: A Handbook for Personal Spiritual Renewal
Edited by Rabbi Kerry M. Olitzky and Rabbi Daniel Judson
6 x 9, 272 pp, Illus., Quality PB, 978-1-58023-169-5 **$18.95**

The Sacred Art of Lovingkindness: Preparing to Practice
By Rabbi Rami Shapiro 5½ x 8½, 176 pp, Quality PB, 978-1-59473-151-8 **$16.99**
(A book from SkyLight Paths, Jewish Lights' sister imprint)

Science Fiction / Mystery & Detective Fiction

Criminal Kabbalah: An Intriguing Anthology of Jewish Mystery & Detective Fiction
Edited by Lawrence W. Raphael; Foreword by Laurie R. King
All-new stories from twelve of today's masters of mystery and detective fiction—sure to delight mystery buffs of all faith traditions.
6 x 9, 256 pp, Quality PB, 978-1-58023-109-1 **$16.95**

Mystery Midrash: An Anthology of Jewish Mystery & Detective Fiction
Edited by Lawrence W. Raphael; Preface by Joel Siegel
6 x 9, 304 pp, Quality PB, 978-1-58023-055-1 **$16.95**

Wandering Stars: An Anthology of Jewish Fantasy & Science Fiction
Edited by Jack Dann; Introduction by Isaac Asimov
6 x 9, 272 pp, Quality PB, 978-1-58023-005-6 **$18.99**

More Wandering Stars: An Anthology of Outstanding Stories of Jewish Fantasy and Science Fiction
Edited by Jack Dann; Introduction by Isaac Asimov
6 x 9, 192 pp, Quality PB, 978-1-58023-063-6 **$16.95**

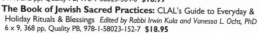

Inspiration

God of Me: Imagining God throughout Your Lifetime
By Rabbi David Lyon Helps you cut through preconceived ideas of God and dogmas that stifle your creativity when thinking about your personal relationship with God. 6 x 9, 176 pp, Quality PB, 978-1-58023-452-8 **$16.99**

The God Upgrade: Finding Your 21st-Century Spirituality in Judaism's 5,000-Year-Old Tradition *By Rabbi Jamie Korngold; Foreword by Rabbi Harold M. Schulweis* A provocative look at how our changing God concepts have shaped every aspect of Judaism. 6 x 9, 176 pp, Quality PB, 978-1-58023-443-6 **$15.99**

The Seven Questions You're Asked in Heaven: Reviewing and Renewing Your Life on Earth *By Dr. Ron Wolfson* An intriguing and entertaining resource for living a life that matters. 6 x 9, 176 pp, Quality PB, 978-1-58023-407-8 **$16.99**

Happiness and the Human Spirit: The Spirituality of Becoming the Best You Can Be *By Rabbi Abraham J. Twerski, MD*
Shows you that true happiness is attainable once you stop looking outside yourself for the source. 6 x 9, 176 pp, Quality PB, 978-1-58023-404-7 **$16.99**; HC, 978-1-58023-343-9 **$19.99**

A Formula for Proper Living: Practical Lessons from Life and Torah
By Rabbi Abraham J. Twerski, MD 6 x 9, 144 pp, HC, 978-1-58023-402-3 **$19.99**

The Bridge to Forgiveness: Stories and Prayers for Finding God and Restoring Wholeness *By Rabbi Karyn D. Kedar* 6 x 9, 176 pp, Quality PB, 978-1-58023-451-1 **$16.99**

The Empty Chair: Finding Hope and Joy—Timeless Wisdom from a Hasidic Master, Rebbe Nachman of Breslov *Adapted by Moshe Mykoff and the Breslov Research Institute* 4 x 6, 128 pp, Deluxe PB w/ flaps, 978-1-879045-67-5 **$9.99**

The Gentle Weapon: Prayers for Everyday and Not-So-Everyday Moments— Timeless Wisdom from the Teachings of the Hasidic Master, Rebbe Nachman of Breslov *Adapted by Moshe Mykoff and S. C. Mizrahi, together with the Breslov Research Institute* 4 x 6, 144 pp, Deluxe PB w/ flaps, 978-1-58023-022-3 **$9.99**

God Whispers: Stories of the Soul, Lessons of the Heart *By Rabbi Karyn D. Kedar* 6 x 9, 176 pp, Quality PB, 978-1-58023-088-9 **$15.95**

God's To-Do List: 103 Ways to Be an Angel and Do God's Work on Earth *By Dr. Ron Wolfson* 6 x 9, 144 pp, Quality PB, 978-1-58023-301-9 **$16.99**

Jewish Stories from Heaven and Earth: Inspiring Tales to Nourish the Heart and Soul *Edited by Rabbi Dov Peretz Elkins* 6 x 9, 304 pp, Quality PB, 978-1-58023-363-7 **$16.99**

Life's Daily Blessings: Inspiring Reflections on Gratitude and Joy for Every Day, Based on Jewish Wisdom *By Rabbi Kerry M. Olitzky* 4½ x 6½, 368 pp, Quality PB, 978-1-58023-396-5 **$16.99**

Restful Reflections: Nighttime Inspiration to Calm the Soul, Based on Jewish Wisdom *By Rabbi Kerry M. Olitzky and Rabbi Lori Forman-Jacobi* 5 x 8, 352 pp, Quality PB, 978-1-58023-091-9 **$16.99**

Sacred Intentions: Morning Inspiration to Strengthen the Spirit, Based on Jewish Wisdom *By Rabbi Kerry M. Olitzky and Rabbi Lori Forman-Jacobi* 4½ x 6½, 448 pp, Quality PB, 978-1-58023-061-2 **$16.99**

Kabbalah / Mysticism

Jewish Mysticism and the Spiritual Life: Classical Texts, Contemporary Reflections *Edited by Dr. Lawrence Fine, Dr. Eitan Fishbane and Rabbi Or N. Rose* Inspirational and thought-provoking materials for contemplation, discussion and action. 6 x 9, 256 pp, HC, 978-1-58023-434-4 **$24.99**

Ehyeh: A Kabbalah for Tomorrow
By Rabbi Arthur Green, PhD 6 x 9, 224 pp, Quality PB, 978-1-58023-213-5 **$18.99**

The Gift of Kabbalah: Discovering the Secrets of Heaven, Renewing Your Life on Earth *By Tamar Frankiel, PhD* 6 x 9, 256 pp, Quality PB, 978-1-58023-141-1 **$16.95**

Seek My Face: A Jewish Mystical Theology *By Rabbi Arthur Green, PhD* 6 x 9, 304 pp, Quality PB, 978-1-58023-130-5 **$19.95**

Zohar: Annotated & Explained *Translation & Annotation by Dr. Daniel C. Matt; Foreword by Andrew Harvey* 5½ x 8½, 176 pp, Quality PB, 978-1-893361-51-5 **$16.99**
(A book from SkyLight Paths, Jewish Lights' sister imprint)

See also *The Way Into Jewish Mystical Tradition* in The Way Into... Series.

Spirituality

The Jewish Lights Spirituality Handbook: A Guide to Understanding, Exploring & Living a Spiritual Life *Edited by Stuart M. Matlins*
What exactly is "Jewish" about spirituality? How do I make it a part of my life? Fifty of today's foremost spiritual leaders share their ideas and experience with us.
6 x 9, 456 pp, Quality PB, 978-1-58023-093-3 **$19.99**

The Sabbath Soul: Mystical Reflections on the Transformative Power of Holy Time *Selection, Translation and Commentary by Eitan Fishbane, PhD*
Explores the writings of mystical masters of Hasidism. Provides translations and interpretations of a wide range of Hasidic sources previously unavailable in English that reflect the spiritual transformation that takes place on the seventh day.
6 x 9, 208 pp, Quality PB, 978-1-58023-459-7 **$18.99**

Repentance: The Meaning and Practice of *Teshuvah*
By Dr. Louis E. Newman; Foreword by Rabbi Harold M. Schulweis; Preface by Rabbi Karyn D. Kedar
Examines both the practical and philosophical dimensions of *teshuvah*, Judaism's core religious-moral teaching on repentance, and its value for us—Jews and non-Jews alike—today. 6 x 9, 256 pp, HC, 978-1-58023-426-9 **$24.99**

Aleph-Bet Yoga: Embodying the Hebrew Letters for Physical and Spiritual Well-Being
By Steven A. Rapp; Foreword by Tamar Frankiel, PhD, and Judy Greenfeld; Preface by Hart Lazer
7 x 10, 128 pp, b/w photos, Quality PB, Lay-flat binding, 978-1-58023-162-6 **$16.95**

A Book of Life: Embracing Judaism as a Spiritual Practice
By Rabbi Michael Strassfeld 6 x 9, 544 pp, Quality PB, 978-1-58023-247-0 **$19.99**

Bringing the Psalms to Life: How to Understand and Use the Book of Psalms
By Rabbi Daniel F. Polish, PhD 6 x 9, 208 pp, Quality PB, 978-1-58023-157-2 **$16.95**

Does the Soul Survive? A Jewish Journey to Belief in Afterlife, Past Lives & Living with Purpose *By Rabbi Elie Kaplan Spitz; Foreword by Brian L. Weiss, MD*
6 x 9, 288 pp, Quality PB, 978-1-58023-165-7 **$18.99**

Entering the Temple of Dreams: Jewish Prayers, Movements and Meditations for the End of the Day *By Tamar Frankiel, PhD, and Judy Greenfeld*
7 x 10, 192 pp, illus., Quality PB, 978-1-58023-079-7 **$16.95**

First Steps to a New Jewish Spirit: Reb Zalman's Guide to Recapturing the Intimacy & Ecstasy in Your Relationship with God *By Rabbi Zalman M. Schachter-Shalomi with Donald Gropman* 6 x 9, 144 pp, Quality PB, 978-1-58023-182-4 **$16.95**

Foundations of Sephardic Spirituality: The Inner Life of Jews of the Ottoman Empire
By Rabbi Marc D. Angel, PhD 6 x 9, 224 pp, Quality PB, 978-1-58023-341-5 **$18.99**

God & the Big Bang: Discovering Harmony between Science & Spirituality
By Dr. Daniel C. Matt 6 x 9, 216 pp, Quality PB, 978-1-879045-89-7 **$18.99**

God in Our Relationships: Spirituality between People from the Teachings of Martin Buber *By Rabbi Dennis S. Ross* 5½ x 8½, 160 pp, Quality PB, 978-1-58023-147-3 **$16.95**

Judaism, Physics and God: Searching for Sacred Metaphors in a Post-Einstein World
By Rabbi David W. Nelson 6 x 9, 352 pp, Quality PB, inc. reader's discussion guide, 978-1-58023-306-4 **$18.99**; HC, 352 pp, 978-1-58023-252-4 **$24.99**

Meaning & Mitzvah: Daily Practices for Reclaiming Judaism through Prayer, God, Torah, Hebrew, Mitzvot and Peoplehood *By Rabbi Goldie Milgram*
7 x 9, 336 pp, Quality PB, 978-1-58023-256-2 **$19.99**

Minding the Temple of the Soul: Balancing Body, Mind, and Spirit through Traditional Jewish Prayer, Movement, and Meditation *By Tamar Frankiel, PhD, and Judy Greenfeld*
7 x 10, 184 pp, Illus., Quality PB, 978-1-879045-64-4 **$18.99**

One God Clapping: The Spiritual Path of a Zen Rabbi *By Rabbi Alan Lew with Sherril Jaffe*
5½ x 8½, 336 pp, Quality PB, 978-1-58023-115-2 **$16.95**

The Soul of the Story: Meetings with Remarkable People
By Rabbi David Zeller 6 x 9, 288 pp, HC, 978-1-58023-272-2 **$21.99**

Tanya, the Masterpiece of Hasidic Wisdom: Selections Annotated & Explained
Translation & Annotation by Rabbi Rami Shapiro; Foreword by Rabbi Zalman M. Schachter-Shalomi
5½ x 8½, 240 pp, Quality PB, 978-1-59473-275-1 **$16.99**

These Are the Words, 2nd Edition: A Vocabulary of Jewish Spiritual Life
By Rabbi Arthur Green, PhD 6 x 9, 320 pp, Quality PB, 978-1-58023-494-8 **$19.99**

Spirituality / Prayer

Making Prayer Real: Leading Jewish Spiritual Voices on Why Prayer Is Difficult and What to Do about It *By Rabbi Mike Comins*
A new and different response to the challenges of Jewish prayer, with "best prayer practices" from Jewish spiritual leaders of all denominations.
6 x 9, 320 pp, Quality PB, 978-1-58023-417-7 **$18.99**

Witnesses to the One: The Spiritual History of the *Sh'ma*
By Rabbi Joseph B. Meszler; Foreword by Rabbi Elyse Goldstein
6 x 9, 176 pp, Quality PB, 978-1-58023-400-9 **$16.99**; HC, 978-1-58023-309-5 **$19.99**

My People's Prayer Book Series: Traditional Prayers, Modern Commentaries *Edited by Rabbi Lawrence A. Hoffman, PhD*
Provides diverse and exciting commentary to the traditional liturgy. Will help you find new wisdom in Jewish prayer, and bring liturgy into your life. Each book includes Hebrew text, modern translations and commentaries from all perspectives of the Jewish world.

Vol. 1—The *Sh'ma* and Its Blessings
   7 x 10, 168 pp, HC, 978-1-879045-79-8 **$29.99**
Vol. 2—The *Amidah* 7 x 10, 240 pp, HC, 978-1-879045-80-4 **$24.95**
Vol. 3—*P'sukei D'zimrah* (Morning Psalms)
   7 x 10, 240 pp, HC, 978-1-879045-81-1 **$29.99**
Vol. 4—*Seder K'riat Hatorah* (The Torah Service)
   7 x 10, 264 pp, HC, 978-1-879045-82-8 **$29.99**
Vol. 5—*Birkhot Hashachar* (Morning Blessings)
   7 x 10, 240 pp, HC, 978-1-879045-83-5 **$24.95**
Vol. 6—*Tachanun* and Concluding Prayers
   7 x 10, 240 pp, HC, 978-1-879045-84-2 **$24.95**
Vol. 7—Shabbat at Home 7 x 10, 240 pp, HC, 978-1-879045-85-9 **$24.95**
Vol. 8—*Kabbalat Shabbat* (Welcoming Shabbat in the Synagogue)
   7 x 10, 240 pp, HC, 978-1-58023-121-3 **$24.99**
Vol. 9—Welcoming the Night: *Minchah* and *Ma'ariv* (Afternoon and Evening Prayer) 7 x 10, 272 pp, HC, 978-1-58023-262-3 **$24.99**
Vol. 10—Shabbat Morning: *Shacharit* and *Musaf* (Morning and Additional Services) 7 x 10, 240 pp, HC, 978-1-58023-240-1 **$29.99**

Spirituality / Lawrence Kushner

I'm God; You're Not: Observations on Organized Religion & Other Disguises of the Ego
6 x 9, 256 pp, Quality PB, 978-1-58023-513-6 **$18.99**; HC, 978-1-58023-441-2 **$21.99**

The Book of Letters: A Mystical Hebrew Alphabet
Popular HC Edition, 6 x 9, 80 pp, 2-color text, 978-1-879045-00-2 **$24.95**
Collector's Limited Edition, 9 x 12, 80 pp, gold-foil-embossed pages, w/ limited-edition silkscreened print, 978-1-879045-04-0 **$349.00**

The Book of Miracles: A Young Person's Guide to Jewish Spiritual Awareness
6 x 9, 96 pp, 2-color illus., HC, 978-1-879045-78-1 **$16.95** *For ages 9–13*

The Book of Words: Talking Spiritual Life, Living Spiritual Talk
6 x 9, 160 pp, Quality PB, 978-1-58023-020-9 **$18.99**

Eyes Remade for Wonder: A Lawrence Kushner Reader *Introduction by Thomas Moore*
6 x 9, 240 pp, Quality PB, 978-1-58023-042-1 **$18.95**

God Was in This Place & I, i Did Not Know: Finding Self, Spirituality and Ultimate Meaning 6 x 9, 192 pp, Quality PB, 978-1-879045-33-0 **$16.95**

Honey from the Rock: An Introduction to Jewish Mysticism
6 x 9, 176 pp, Quality PB, 978-1-58023-073-5 **$16.95**

Invisible Lines of Connection: Sacred Stories of the Ordinary
5½ x 8½, 160 pp, Quality PB, 978-1-879045-98-9 **$16.99**

Jewish Spirituality: A Brief Introduction for Christians
5½ x 8½, 112 pp, Quality PB, 978-1-58023-150-3 **$12.95**

The River of Light: Jewish Mystical Awareness
6 x 9, 192 pp, Quality PB, 978-1-58023-096-4 **$18.99**

The Way Into Jewish Mystical Tradition
6 x 9, 224 pp, Quality PB, 978-1-58023-200-5 **$18.99**; HC, 978-1-58023-029-2 **$21.95**

About Jewish Lights

People of all faiths and backgrounds yearn for books that attract, engage, educate, and spiritually inspire.

Our principal goal is to stimulate thought and help all people learn about who the Jewish People are, where they come from, and what the future can be made to hold. While people of our diverse Jewish heritage are the primary audience, our books speak to people in the Christian world as well and will broaden their understanding of Judaism and the roots of their own faith.

We bring to you authors who are at the forefront of spiritual thought and experience. While each has something different to say, they all say it in a voice that you can hear.

Our books are designed to welcome you and then to engage, stimulate, and inspire. We judge our success not only by whether or not our books are beautiful and commercially successful, but by whether or not they make a difference in your life.

For your information and convenience, at the back of this book we have provided a list of other Jewish Lights books you might find interesting and useful. They cover all the categories of your life:

Bar/Bat Mitzvah
Bible Study / Midrash
Children's Books
Congregation Resources
Current Events / History
Ecology / Environment
Fiction: Mystery, Science Fiction
Grief / Healing
Holidays / Holy Days
Inspiration
Kabbalah / Mysticism / Enneagram

Life Cycle
Meditation
Men's Interest
Parenting
Prayer / Ritual / Sacred Practice
Social Justice
Spirituality
Theology / Philosophy
Travel
Twelve Steps
Women's Interest

Stuart M. Matlins, Publisher

Or phone, fax, mail or e-mail to: **JEWISH LIGHTS Publishing**
Sunset Farm Offices, Route 4 • P.O. Box 237 • Woodstock, Vermont 05091
Tel: (802) 457-4000 • Fax: (802) 457-4004 • www.jewishlights.com
Credit card orders: (800) 962-4544 (8:30AM–5:30PM EST Monday–Friday)
Generous discounts on quantity orders. SATISFACTION GUARANTEED. Prices subject to change.